Winning the
Clutter War

By Sandra Felton

Winning the Clutter War

Sandra Felton

© 2005 by Sandra Felton

Published by Revell
a division of Baker Publishing Group
P.O. Box 6287, Grand Rapids, MI 49516-6287
www.revellbooks.com

Spire edition published 2010
ISBN 978-0-8007-8809-4

Previously published in 2005 as *The Messies Manual*

Printed in the United States of America

Unless otherwise indicated, Scripture is taken from the King James Version of the Bible.

Scripture marked NIV is taken from the Holy Bible, New International Version®, NIV®. Copyright © 1973, 1978, 1984 by Biblica, Inc.™ Used by permission of Zondervan. All rights reserved worldwide. www.zondervan.com

The quote from "Happy Talk" (*South Pacific*) is copyright © 1949 by Richard Rodgers and Oscar Hammerstein. Copyright renewed, Williamson Music Co., owner of publication and allied rights for the Western Hemisphere and Japan. International copyright secured. All rights reserved. Used by permission.

10   11   12   13   14   15   16   7   6   5   4   3   2   1

To my mother, Seco Haley,
whose example kept me striving
for a better way of life
when it was difficult to remember
that another way existed.

When it comes to keeping an orderly house, no one is hopeless—not even you! So, go and dig up a pencil (try looking behind the hutch—one rolled under there two years ago) and evaluate yourself by identifying your particular strengths and weaknesses. True or false:

I am successful in using coupons.

I still have my high school dance program.

I plan my meals while I shop.

I know how much I have in my checking account.

I keep my bedroom door closed when I have guests.

There's more! For your score on this probing survey, see chapter 11.

If you're longing to welcome unexpected guests with open arms (instead of hiding behind a stack of newspapers) . . . if you're tired of fighting an avalanche every time you open a closet or cabinet door . . . if there's a "Cleanie" inside of you who's striving to break free, then *Winning the Clutter War* will provide you with the humorous, helpful guidance and painless, practical tips you need to forever break away from chronic messiness!

Contents

Contents

Foreword

Long, Long Ago . . .

This is my story that began over twenty-five years ago. I feared I was doomed to live and die struggling with clutter in my home and disorder in my life. It is the story of how I changed and later helped many others change with me. The desperate condition of my life before I changed is described in chapter 2, "Confessions of a Reformed Messie." My strategy for change is described in chapter 12, "The Mt. Vernon Method: How I Took Command" so I won't go into the details now.

When I found help for myself and felt the drive to clutter leave my heart and life like a fever breaking, I instinctively wanted to share with others, although I was not sure that there were any others who were drowning in clutter as I was.

So back in 1981 I put a little public service announcement in the *Miami Herald*—"Messy house? Frustrated? Come to Messies Anonymous." I gave the location and evening meeting time. Since I was afraid to sit alone in the dark, I asked a friend to wait with me in a back building of our church. I was not sure anybody would show up. I suspected I was the only one in the world who had this problem. Who could know!

Waiting in the Darkness

On that first night my friend and I sat together in that little building in a mango grove with the darkness closing in around us, waiting and wondering. Down the unpaved pathway, lights from approaching cars began to appear, mostly late. Twelve people arrived. We were a brave group but shellshocked from the impact of our problem. I recall one man was about to have his business evicted by the fire marshall. Week after week we hammered out and applied the plans that appear in this book. And slowly we changed, as you will too.

Early on in the process, a reporter for the *Miami Herald* wrote a story about our group. The article was distributed by a large national news service to many of the major newspapers in the country. Twelve thousand letters poured in pleading for help, often adding "Hurry!" This book, *The Messies Manual*, was written to answer their cry.

At first I printed copies of the book myself to sell to those who asked for help. Two years later Revell began publishing and distributing *The Messies Manual* in a way I couldn't. Since then they have published many of my other books. These books were written to flesh out the program and answer other questions about how to change.

The Message Spreads

In the twenty-plus years since that little group met, the program hammered out there has spread all over the world to English-speaking countries such as Canada, South Africa, Australia, New Zealand, and England. Books in German have become bestsellers, and many German groups have been formed. The word "messie" has entered the German word pool. Books have been translated into Spanish and Dutch, and the Chinese have bought rights to translate and publish. Through newspapers, magazines, radio programs, television, and book distribution, the message of hope has spread to women and men around the world. The program has jumped cultural lines. Cluttering is an equal-opportunity problem and no respecter of social position, intelligence, or any other characteristic.

Local Messies Anonymous groups have formed, and there are many successful and active online support groups. Other help is available through the website www.messies.com for English speakers. There are also websites that serve German and Spanish speakers.

There are no leaders in the group. There are no dues. There are no professionals who benefit from the organization directly. Our members are mostly women, though men are surely welcome. Anyone who suffers from chronic disorganization is welcome. We call that person by the gentle name of Messie, and it is Anonymous because we don't necessarily want outsiders to know our problem.

Since the beginning of Messies Anonymous, much has been done to help individuals overcome disorganization. The National Association of Professional Organizers and the National Study Group on Chronic Disorganization have been formed in America. Other professional organizer groups have begun abroad. These offer referrals around the country. Psychologists have turned their attention to the problem, usually focusing on hoarding as an anxiety disorder. All of these offer insights and help.

A Simple Program

Ten years after its beginning, Alcoholics Anonymous extended their twelve steps and twelve traditions to those who wish to use them. Their late adoption made Messies Anonymous something of a hybrid. Some Messies emphasize the steps and others go about change in a different way. The twelve-step program is explained in the book *Hope for the Hopeless Messie*.

Just as Bill W.'s beliefs and background flavored his interpretation of the twelve steps of AA, my background as a Bible-believing Christian flavors the interpretation of the higher power of the twelve steps as God, who is willing to restore us to sanity and tells us about that process in the Bible. As was true with Bill W.'s group, because of the variety of backgrounds of those who come for help, there are a variety of approaches in this area. Controversy over differences occasionally arises. Controversy of any kind only distracts from our focus on solving our problem and seldom is useful to pursue as an issue.

Our program is a simple program but not a simplistic one. Simplistic is naive and inadequate. Simple is enough—but no more. Be assured that you can find help for yourself.

The program worked for me. It didn't come easily or quickly. But little by little as I changed, my house changed. In today's world many Messies who are changing slowly but surely say, "Baby steps, baby steps." I challenged ideas and feelings that had drawn me into clutter. Today I am one grateful person. I did not want to live my whole life in clutter, and I sure didn't want to die with it around me.

But What about You?

So here you are reading this book about organizing because you are one of the growing crowd of those of us in the modern world who struggle with our affluence. We live in crowded and sometimes cluttered houses. We buy sheds and rent storage units because we are exhausted from caring for too much stuff.

The problems and stresses of individuals living with clutter are increasing as affluence proliferates belongings and busy schedules absorb time to handle them. Those who once lived average organized lives find themselves starting to go under.

Maybe you don't consider yourself a candidate to join a group. You don't want to hire outside help at this time. You may not even be interested or ready to go online for more help and information. You just want to live in harmony with your stuff and to manage your time well.

Not to worry. This book is for you. Years of experience have given us insights into the problems and solutions that confront us all in modern life. An expanded program under the name The Organizer Lady brings that rich wisdom to the broader audience. We do hope that those who haven't found answers elsewhere may be able to find it in the pages of this book and will join us on the road to recovery and freedom in the organizing program presented here.

As we say in our meetings, "It works if you work it."

Coming Out of the Dark

Our goal for all of us is to get to the place where our lives are no longer consumed either by living with clutter or by the struggle to get organized and stay that way.

A successfully orderly life looks like this:

- The house is set up to work with us.
- Our routine keeps us moving in the right direction more or less automatically.

- Our habits, thought patterns, and emotions have come under enough control that we no longer have to struggle to keep ourselves from drowning in clutter.

Eventually, if all goes as planned, keeping the house organized will become more or less a non-issue. Though it may never be fully automatic, it can get much easier, even serene.

Wow! That's a thought!

I just love the story of Cinderella. One day Cinderella is living by an unpleasant fireplace dressed in tatters, getting dirty, working hard, never getting out for fun, and receiving no reward for all her effort. She is sad and frustrated. (Does it sound a little like your life?)

The next day she is found by the prince, whisked off to the palace, and lives as a princess in a beautiful castle, never needing to turn her hand to clean house. And she lives happily ever after.

Who brings about this wonderful transformation? Why, it is her fairy godmother, of course!

For years I waited for my fairy godmother to come and wave her magic wand over me and magically change my hovel into a castle—and my frustration into joy.

But she never came.

There is magic to be found, but I was looking in the wrong place for it. The program you are about to begin will work its magic on you. You are about to enter the world of the Messie and the Cleanie. You will learn about the Mount Vernon Method, the Flipper System, and other secrets of housekeeping. Each chapter contains a little magic dust, and when you are finished you will be prepared to become that princess you dream of becoming.

But you must wave the wand. You must sprinkle the magic dust. I know you will, because I know you won't settle for that stool in the cinders once you know there is a castle waiting for you and there is hope of finding it.

I want your home to be a castle, full of beauty and dignity. I want you to be a princess in your own home.

"Oh, no," you protest, "I'm not reading this book to get some kind of magic. I just want to be able to find my shoes, get the piles off the tables, and get my kids off to school with matching socks. I live a practical, mundane life. I just want to survive. I have no time or patience for fairy tales or dreams."

Maybe so. I know you would be satisfied if the house were just under control. This is a very practical book. You will be able to find that order you want.

But maybe, just maybe, after things begin to clear, somewhere in your house you'll find the corner of the castle.

God bless you, Princess.

Introducing the Messie

(As If You Need It!)

Intelligence is the quickness in see-ing things as they are.

GEORGE SANTAYANA

We all know them. They are the people who never seem to get control of their housework and their time, the type who need all day to accomplish nothing. They live in dread of opening a closet door, for fear they will be buried under an avalanche of canned goods, flashlight batteries, tissue boxes, and stockings with only one run that might come in handy someday for something. (Well, you never know.)

A casual visitor to the home of such a person would be in constant danger of tripping over rollerblades, knocking piles of paper to the floor, and stepping on a ten-year-old's pet frog.

But a casual visitor is not likely to get into this person's home. She won't even invite her best friend, not with the house in such a mess.

This type of housekeeper—if that is not too strong a term for a person whose house appears to keep *her*—has a name. She is known as a "Messie."

If you are reading this book, chances are you know her very well indeed, because she is you. Furthermore, you are tired of it. You are ready to take command of your house and your life, if only you can figure out how.

Perhaps, until now, you have felt yourself to be alone. You thought no other person could possibly have a house that looks as if a tornado just struck it. You have not wanted to talk about it, not wanted to do anything that might reveal your secret shame to the world.

Well, take heart, because you are very far from being in a class by yourself. Millions of women—men too—share your problem. And it's curable, or at least controllable.

How to Use This Book

You bought this book because you want change in your house and life. Great! To get the most out of it you have to interact with it. But don't try to do everything in the book at once. Focus on the parts that will bring you the change you want.

Here are a few suggestions for you.

1. As you read, underline. Write in the margins. Get little sticky notes and use them as markers for the parts you will want to find again. Start a project list and a to-do list. Make notations to yourself in the back of the book. Note the things you need to purchase. Try to refrain from marking up the book if you got it from the library. You'll need to go buy your own book. (Lucky for you it's pretty inexpensive.)

2. Concentrate on the basics. Mount Vernon, the Flipper, and the Three S system of organizing, used with persistence, will lift even the most hopeless Messie out of the morass of clutter she has fallen into.

3. Zero in on your special hot spots of need. Adapt the ideas to your life. According to the 80/20 rule, if you find your most important 20 percent of this book, you

are guaranteed to see an 80 percent improvement in your life.

4. Don't stop until you get where you want to be. Maybe the book will not be enough to keep you going. Find a friend or group who can offer the support you need. Get in touch with us through www.messies.com for more help and support.

You have in your hand what you need to know in order to change. Keep going back to it until you really understand what to do and do it.

Messies Anonymous offers help by other books, Messies Anonymous twelve-step support groups, the MA ClutterBuddy program, an interactive website, tapes, and videos. By word of mouth, radio, television, the internet, and printed articles, we let people know help is available. They too can live the life of harmony they yearn for.

PART 1

Help! House Out of Control!

What's Your Messies Quotient (M.Q.)?

To cure anything—a disease, a stutter, an ingrown toenail—you first have to classify it. Try this short test:

Yes	No	
☐	☐	Are all the spoons in your kitchen drawer neatly nested up to one another, while all the pots in the house sit in the sink and sulk? See the Perfectionist Messie.
☐	☐	Did your mother have a "thing" about emptying bathroom wastebaskets? Is yours overflowing into the shower stall? See the Rebellious Messie.
☐	☐	Would you love to come home and read the evening paper? Are there six papers currently residing by your favorite chair? See the Relaxed Messie.
☐	☐	Are you still finding your teenager's baby teeth in the corners of the drawer in your bedside table? See the Sentimental Messie.
☐	☐	Did you toss out your ironing board long ago? See the Spartan Messie.
☐	☐	After your dress comes back from the dry cleaner, does it hang on the back of the kitchen door? See the Clean Messie.
☐	☐	Is it true that a gritty bathtub is less slippery than a sparkling one? See the Safe Messie.
☐	☐	Do you truly believe there is something sinful in serving children a pie from the supermarket? See the Old-Fashioned Messie.
☐	☐	Have you figured out a simple solution to worldwide hunger, while your six-year-old learned to make toast for survival? See the Idealistic Messie.

1

Messies Classified

*We are all self-made, but only
the successful will admit it.*

EARL NIGHTINGALE

Messies have one thing in common: On a scale of 0 to 10 (0 is disaster and 10 is perfection), their housekeeping falls into the 1–3 range.

This, of course, makes them the opposites of the housekeepers we know as "Cleanies," whose efforts are rewarded with a rating in the 7–10 range. It also sets them apart from average housekeepers—those whose homes fall into disarray on occasion, but not often and not for long, and who therefore merit a 4–6 rating.

Aside from their abysmally low housekeeping rating, Messies have little in common. They got to be where they are by different roads, and they have different styles of messiness.

Let us, therefore, take a look at different types of Messies. If you can recognize yourself in one of these word portraits, you will be well on the way to finding a solution to your problem.

The Perfectionist Messie

The Perfectionist Messie has very high standards for individual jobs. The house may be a wreck, but she decides to begin by cleaning the oven. And it is well done, very well done.

If you say, "No one sees the inside of the oven," she takes pride in saying, "But I know it is clean." In the meantime, the whole picture deteriorates.

Here, indecisiveness is cloaked in the guise of perfectionism. Generally this housekeeper cannot decide which approach to putting the house in order would be best. So she decides not to decide. This is a bad decision.

The Rebellious Messie

This Messie has psychological hang-ups from childhood. Mom insisted on cleanliness and order, and now that she is grown, she is going to show independence by defiance.

The tragedy, of course, is to let infantile reactions ruin our own lives and those of our families now that we are adults.

I heard a middle-aged woman say she had procrastinated for years about hanging a mirror even though it was in her way on the floor. The reason she didn't hang it was because the sight of the unhung mirror annoyed her mother, and she derived pleasure from the annoyance it caused. I guess she is showing Mom that Mom can't make her do it. But she is paying a high price for trying to show how grown-up she is.

The Relaxed Messie

The Relaxed Messie rationalizes that the world outside is hostile and home is the place to relax. Why work at home, too?

So things are let go. The result is that when the rationalizer comes home from that high-pressure job, she faces a hostile house. Things assault the eye and clutter life.

How nice it would be to come home to a beautiful, inviting home that says, "Welcome," and invites us to relax! The truth, as any Messie can tell you, is that messiness is not relaxing. It causes strain, pressure, and jangled nerves.

The Sentimental Messie

Every scrap brought home by Johnny is precious. Every shell picked up on a beautiful day is valuable. We must keep our memories. I think memory is the source of the problem here. Some of us Messies have poor memories, so these things are the only way we can remember. When we throw them out, our memories actually are gone. In such cases, I suggest a memory journal. Write down the day's activities, especially the nice ones. These pages will be invaluable not only to you but to your children and grandchildren.

Token remembrances also can be kept, of course, in easy-to-store, labeled plastic shoe boxes. But remember, keep only token items—not everything!

The Sentimental Messie is also a picture-taking Messie. Pictures are another aid to a poor memory. Sometimes we don't even have to have them developed. We just like to know they are available for some time when we might get them developed. So in virtually every drawer in the house, undeveloped film can be found. One woman said she had her film developed so late that she did not recognize the people standing with her in the picture.

Perhaps no characteristic of Messies has such a hold as this one. Sentimentality is not a bad thing if it is not overdone or misapplied. But we frequently do both. When the belongings from our past begin to pile up in an unpleasant way in our present and adversely affect our future, it's time to jettison them. (Gasp! Is that possible?)

You will find tactics to deal with many of the sentimental items in your life in chapter 22. But the underlying way to let go of the past is to shift your gaze to your life in today's world. Plan for a wonderful future. Don't let anything keep you from accomplishing your best vision for your life.

The Spartan Messie

The Spartan Messie has a special approach to the difficulties of housekeeping. The ancient Spartans lived with only the necessities of life. Similarly, it may occur to a Messie that if there were less to care for, or if it were somehow shut up or nailed down and not used, it would be possible to handle it.

The next step is to see what can be eliminated: "Let's see, I could always have one-pot dinners so I would have just one pot to wash. I could have one set of sheets so I'd just have to wash them and put them back on the bed, which would eliminate folding them or having them lie around in a basket. Or better still, I could make up the bed and sleep on top of the spread. That would eliminate washing sheets and bed making. I could clean up some of the other rooms and not use them anymore, just put a velvet rope across each door."

How often do Americans change the sheets on their beds? According to a recent survey:

Once a week—51%
Twice a week—31%
Once a month—12%
Less than once a month—2%

And so, to some degree or another, they cut out the things they have to handle. As a rule they don't actually get rid of them, they just exclude them from their care.

The Clean Messie

As long as things are clean, Clean Messies reason, they can be left out. This is why clean clothes are left in the basket and not folded. (After all, they are clean, and that's the main thing.) The dishes are washed and left out on the counter. But they are clean. Isn't that what counts?

The Safe Messie

The Safe Messie leaves the bed unmade, "because it can air out better, and that kills more germs." The floors are not waxed, "because they might be slippery and dangerous." The dishes are not dried by hand, "because the germs from the dishcloth might get on the dishes. Air drying is more sanitary."

And finally, "I can't have a maid, because she might have a boyfriend who is a thief, and I'll be robbed." One cannot be too careful, after all.

The trouble with all these ways of thinking is that they tie us up and reduce our options for keeping the house the way we want it.

The Old-Fashioned Messie

For some reason, there are people who just enjoy doing things the old-fashioned way. For them, the only good way is the old way. This is a definite matter of principle—though it is hard to know what the reason is.

This might mean our Old-Fashioned Messie will have as a principle that the only way to do the floor is on her hands and knees with a brush. Now actually, the floor never gets done that way because it is too much work. But believe me, if it ever did get done, it would be done right. Their motto is "Do it right—or not at all." A lot of time it turns out "not at all."

Some other ideas the Old-Fashioned Messie may have are to bake pies and cakes from scratch instead of using a mix, to wax and buff the wooden floor with a cloth instead of a buffer, to beat the rug instead of vacuuming, or use cloth instead of disposable diapers. It's not that some of these things aren't appropriate sometimes, but to do things the hard way just because it is an old-fashioned way is a hindrance to progress in housekeeping.

The Idealistic Messie

The Idealistic Messie's head is in the clouds. Great thoughts and ideas are what interest this Messie.

But the results are disastrous to an idealist. The beauty and charm, the satisfying family life, all melt under the heat of the messy home. The idealist, attuned to greater things, seldom notices the relationship between the messy house and the fading dreams.

In short, no matter what type of Messie you are, it's an unsatisfying life.

2

Confessions of a Reformed Messie

*Compared to what we ought to be and
can be, we are only half awake.*

WILLIAM JAMES

My mother was a Cleanie. What a marvelous thing it was in those days of my youth always to have a clean, beautiful house to come home to!

Keeping house seemed to come naturally to her. My drawers were always neat, my room in order. I functioned in the order she created. She did try to train me, her only daughter. What a discouragement it must have been for her! I took to housekeeping like a cat to water.

We had spells when she did her best to get me in the groove and other spells when she gave up and found it easier to do it herself. In the meantime, I had other things of greater consequence to do.

In high school there was schoolwork. To me, studying was heady stuff. I worked on developing writing skills by turning out short stories and poetry. I took art lessons after school and was tutored privately in French. Who in the world cared if there was dust on the table legs with art and philosophy hovering so excitingly close?

Then I went to college, had a career as a junior high school math teacher, and married a minister. I was on my own with a house to keep. That's when I first noticed something seriously amiss. I found that the well-kept look, which had seemed to come effortlessly to my mother, didn't come to me at all.

At first I blamed the houses. The first one was too little. The next one was too big. I was sure there was just some small adjustment I needed to make in my situation and things would be all right. I was still busy with other, more important things. My husband was pastoring churches, and I was involved in his work. The children came, and I reacted to the housework. But I never controlled it.

Newton's second law of thermodynamics states that anything, left to itself, tends toward disorganization. This is especially true with houses. Felton's law is, "Any house left to keep itself tends to disaster." Murphy's law applied to housekeeping is, "Any mess that can happen, will."

It's tough being a Messie and a minister's wife. People like to drop around, especially if you are living in the parsonage right next door to the church.

Ivan's first church was in the northern Indiana farm region. Of Southern stock, I had grown up in Tennessee with its real or imagined tradition of frail womanhood.

These Indiana women were heartier than I was. They never even considered the concept of a "lady of leisure."

I once heard a parishioner talk about having done her spring cleaning. I was amazed that as part of it she had varnished the windowsills with marine varnish. Most of the women in the parish sewed, canned, had gardens, ran tractors, did church work, and kept neat homes, while I just wandered around trying to keep my head above water wondering what was wrong.

These women were gracious and never mentioned the gap between my abilities and theirs, which I felt so keenly. The worst part was that I could not figure out why they were succeeding and I was not.

In those days, as a young mother, I was able to tell myself that there was a *reason* for my poor housekeeping. More babies came, giving me further reasons. I was feeling better about my messiness now that I had collected so many good reasons. A really good excuse is a valuable thing. Several good excuses are a treasure.

The excuses satisfied my mind somewhat, but the soul is not so easily quieted. The frustration of not being able to find things, the embarrassment of having company drop in without warning, the hard work that never gets anywhere—there is no way to make these things somehow all right. They sap the joy from life.

It's really tough being a Messie.

---

excuse ik-'skyüs n. A perfectly reasonable explanation for the fact that your husband can't find the monthly bills . . . or the checkbook . . . or one pen that hasn't gone dry because someone left the top off for two weeks.

3

A "Messies" Quiz

*Not everything you face can be changed, but
everything you change must first be faced.*

Test your knowledge of the problems of messiness by taking
this quiz. Are the following statements true or false?

1. Trying to be in control of life motivates Messies to collect
   too much.
2. Before they can begin to change, Messies must release
   the grandiose attitude that they can handle multitudes
   of things, projects, opportunities, etc.
3. If Messies develop proper attitudes about organizing,
   keeping an orderly house will be a breeze.
4. The idea of eliminating old destructive ways of thinking
   and nonproductive ways of doing things makes Messies
   nervous.
5. If Messies change too much, they will lose their unique
   personality.
6. Living a serene and orderly life feels wonderful to the
   reforming Messie.

7. Messies are less productive when they get more organized.
8. Messies lack basic internal organizational skills.
9. Organized people need and use more organizational systems than disorganized people.
10. Messies should throw away stacks of old papers without looking at each piece of paper.
11. Because they love to keep papers, Messies love to file things.
12. Messies don't mind living in a disorganized way.
13. Messies lack appropriate boundaries in their lives.
14. Messies don't like to plan ahead in detail.

Let's see how well you have done. Although you know a lot about Messies, some of the answers may surprise you.

1. Trying to be in control of life motivates Messies to collect too much.

This is true. We start out wanting so much to get everything under control and we end up losing control in a big way. Messies try to:

- be too perfect
- do too much
- know too much
- take care of too many people
- have too many interests
- enjoy too much
- remember too much
- save things in case somebody else might need them someday

2. *Before they can begin to change, Messies must release the grandiose attitude that they can handle multitudes of things, projects, opportunities, etc.*

This is also true. In short, Messies try to be superhuman. But we aren't. Bill W., founder of Alcoholics Anonymous, said, "First of all, we had to quit playing God. It didn't work." Often we are not aware of this tendency because it has been so much a natural part of our thinking for so long. Once that inflated idea begins to release its grip on our lives, we will be able to release our grip on all the other ideas that compel us to live a messy life.

3. *If Messies develop proper attitudes about organizing, keeping an orderly house will be a breeze.*

Ah, if it were that simple! The answer is false. Changing our basic way of thinking is the important first step, but it will never be easy. There are other factors such as distractibility, difficulty in categorizing, memory deficits, and other problems that we need to deal with. But, using techniques designed to handle these other problems, and being willing to make the change in our basic idea that we can control too much, we will be on that wonderful road of recovery.

Our houses will change as we do.

4. *The idea of eliminating old destructive ways of thinking and nonproductive ways of doing things makes Messies nervous.*

You betcha! It's really hard to do what we need to do to get out of this pickle. Messies may not like what those destructive ideas, feelings, and behaviors do to their organizational lives, but they are comfortable with the qualities that make them unique.

They even get used to the adrenaline rush and excitement that the chaotic Messie lifestyle brings with it.

5. If Messies change too much, they will lose their unique personality.

Nothing could be farther from reality. This is definitely false. In actuality, people cannot make enough changes to interfere with the core of who they are. You will always be uniquely you. Even though Messies will always need to keep somewhat more stuff and to seek the stimulation of more activities than the average person, experience tells us that in order to really enjoy and more fully express our wonderful uniqueness, we must modify our natural bent toward "too much."

6. Living a serene and orderly life feels wonderful to the reforming Messie.

This is a hard one. Sometimes it is true and sometimes it is false. During the struggle to simplify and organize, emotions ride a roller coaster. At first, there is a sense of relief when we realize we can begin to get rid of things and organize them. As we begin to live the new, more serene life, we begin to feel uncomfortable. We may even be tempted to sabotage our serenity. But by committing to basic organizational changes and returning to them when we get off track, we will eventually get to the point that we are grateful, so very, very grateful, for being delivered from the grip of the former way of life.

7. Messies are less productive when they get more organized.

This is probably not true. Although the Messie may be doing, keeping, and attempting less, actual productivity probably goes up because the Messie does not waste so much time looking for stuff and because she follows through and finishes more of the projects she begins. At first Messies may get less done because of the newness. But when they get used to working in an organized environment, production goes way up. Getting out from under the mess frees the Messie to get more done.

8. Messies lack basic internal organizational skills.

Well, I hate to tell you this, but it is pretty much true. We just don't have the natural ability to play the organizing game well. Ability to organize is a natural skill, similar to playing basketball or singing or spelling.

Randy Frost, who with other researchers has done several important studies on the subject of hoarding, says that Messies who keep too much have "more complex concepts." He explains that "their concepts are more detailed and require more information for decision making." While this seems flattering in a way and confirms a sneaking suspicion that I have always had that Messies are a cut above others in intelligence, we run into problems because of this characteristic. A Messie professional (who had a Ph.D. by the way) once expressed it by saying that she could not make decisions because she saw so many sides of every decision to be made.

9. Organized people need and use more organizational systems than disorganized people.

This is false. The irony is that disorganized people need to learn to overorganize themselves in order to function. Organized people seem to float right along without all the helps we need. I'm sure my organized friends think I am crazy because of all the boxes, signs, and organizational systems I have built into my life to compensate for my forgetfulness, my difficulty in categorizing, distractibility, and the like. But I'm grateful for these systems, and I need them to function.

10. Messies should throw away stacks of old papers without looking at each piece of paper.

There is a special phenomenon that may make this unwise. Messies consistently tend to mix stock certificates, checks, cash, personal documents, and other important papers in with old newspapers, ads for sales long ago, and other worthless papers. I suspect this happens because of an attention deficit that "hits" when they have the important paper in their hand and they put it down without realizing it. Or it may be that because they can't decide where to put this very important paper and they have no organizational system to hold it, they procrastinate by putting it in that famous pile (or piles) to get back to when they "have more time."

What a job these piles become! Handling them would bring even the most enthusiastic and skillfully efficient person to his or her organizational knees. And here we are working on those piles!

11. Because they love to keep papers, Messies love to file things.

On the whole, this statement is false. Messies have a love/hate relationship with filing cabinets. They love the idea that they can keep lots of stuff in a small space. But they are afraid that if they put their important papers (and they are all important) into the file, the papers will be forever lost. They have had this awful thing happen. So they try to design other methods using trays or stacks with colored dividers in order to avoid the filing cabinet.

But filing is by far the method of choice for keeping large quantities of paper. I have twenty file drawers of paper and have designed a method I share later in this book that works for me like a charm. I could not function without it. Those of us who are Messies can learn to use filing cabinets with success, but we must adjust the system to meet our needs.

12. Messies don't mind living in a disorganized way.

Most Messies wish they were not burdened with the problems of clutter. We all know Messies like Aunt Sue, who doesn't seem to mind being disorganized. She happily moves things off the couch to give you a seat and shows you her home-canned goods stacked all around the kitchen and dining room.

This is probably a testimony to Aunt Sue's cheerful disposition and the fact that she has come to terms with the mess since she does not know any way out. However, if she found a way out, she would probably be the happiest and most grateful reformed Messie you have ever seen.

In contrast to the happy Messie we see, there are scores living under stress behind closed doors. They don't like what they have done to themselves. They don't even quite know how it happened or what to do about it.

Messies tend to get blindsided by their own special qualities. "It's like a baby tiger," said John, an anonymous Messie. "It starts out innocent enough, but later you look around and it is out of control."

13. Messies lack appropriate boundaries in their lives.

This is definitely true. Much of the creative strength of Messies is their willingness to go beyond the boundaries of ordinary thinking. But this valuable ability that helps them in their creative productivity does not work when applied in other areas of life. Messies lack appropriate boundaries in several areas.

They fail to consider lack of space, i.e., that space has boundaries. They keep buying books without considering there is no place to put them.

They don't notice where their responsibility leaves off in relation to other people. They keep trying to inappropriately take care of everybody else's needs.

They mingle themselves with their possessions in such a way that when they get rid of their belongings they feel as though they are losing a part of themselves. They also feel that the possessions of other people have a little of those people in the possessions.

They blur time boundaries in that they try to live in the past, present, and future all at the same time.

14. Messies don't like to plan ahead in detail.

This is true. Messies like to decide impulsively based on their mood at the time. This results in disorganization in many ways.

One reason people keep so much stuff is so that they will have what they need for spur-of-the-moment decisions. They take more clothes on a trip than they need so they can wear what "feels" right when they are beginning to get dressed. They don't like to lock themselves in to a time schedule so they can go with their emotional flow from moment to moment. The idea of deciding ahead on a purely intellectual basis does not seem quite right to them. They procrastinate as long as possible to see how their mood is going.

Messies strongly respect their emotional urges. Somewhere, way in the back of their minds, they question whether they should do an activity in which their heart is not involved. Cleaning may be delayed until the mood to clean becomes strong. If the urge to shop or create or whatever comes over them, they honor it.

Everybody has to plan ahead. But Messies like to plan with more flexibility built in. Messies are often highly productive, successful people, but they do it on their own terms. "Their own terms" often has a lot of craziness built in and causes them problems with both clutter and time management.

Knowing these things about the Messie personality can give freedom to all of us who recognize that the way we function has caused us to have a messy house. Although it won't be easy, now we have a chance to do something about it. What a relief!

The Good, the Bad, and the Ugly

The trouble with keeping so much stuff is that the really important things get lost in the mediocre stuff.

- Your wedding tape is buried beneath "good" but unimportant tapes.
- Your special headache medicine is missing in action among the other remedies. And you (with a headache) have to search for it!
- Really good, even classic, snapshots that could be family heirlooms are not even recognizable because they are buried under mediocre snapshots you could not bear to discard.

When the bad and the ugly mix in with the good, and the good is lost in the shuffle, the quality of our lives is greatly diminished.

4

Outlooks That Hinder

We have met the enemy, and he is us.

WALT KELLY (*POGO*)

The mind is the key to what we do. Sometimes we slip into a pattern of thinking that hinders us from making progress, and we never realize that while our wills are saying, "Go, go," our minds are saying, "No, no." So we end up failing because we are harboring pet ideas that keep us from going forward. We have to be willing to make some changes in the way we think if we are ever going to make permanent changes in our houses. In this chapter are attitudes that need to be dealt with if we are going to succeed. These may include some of the outlooks you will need to change.

Task Orientation

People who say, "I've got all day to vacuum the rug" are indicating that they are going through the motions of housekeeping and doing the job just to get it done, not because it is an important part of a larger picture. As long as we look at housekeeping as a group of isolated tasks lined up in order to be done, we can put them off because there is no reason to do them except to get them off the list.

The solution is goal orientation rather than task orientation. We should never lose sight of our overall goal, which in this case is a beautiful and orderly house. When we see our work in terms of this goal, individual tasks become a means to an end.

Let's look at it this way: Suppose two people are given two different jigsaw puzzles. The puzzles are identical except that one has a beautiful picture on it that cannot be seen or enjoyed until it is assembled, while the other one has no picture, only gray pieces. If you ask the first person what he is doing he will say, "I am making a beautiful picture." If you ask the second person he will say, "I am fitting together one piece after another. After a while I will have each piece fitted in." The first person is goal oriented; the second is task oriented.

A person who is task oriented can wait all day to vacuum the rug, as long as it gets vacuumed that day. A person who is goal oriented, however, won't wait all day since her goal is to maintain a nice-looking house at all times, and a dirty rug will short-circuit that goal.

The Purely Practical Approach

Why put the toothpaste away if you are going to get it out again in a few hours? Why make the bed just to unmake it that evening? Is it practical to wash a few dishes? Why not wait till you have a whole sink full and do them all at once? These ideas *are* practical, but they delay your reaching your goal—a beautiful house.

The Myth of Creative Disorganization

Everybody knows that creative and intelligent people can be very disorganized. Some creative people are deliberately disorganized. Have you ever seen the sign on a desk that says, "A neat desk is a sign of a sick mind"? This is some disorganized creative person taking the offensive.

Frequently, however, this clutter interferes with the fullest use of the creative gift. Imagine the writer who can't find his paper or research material, or the artist who misplaces supplies. Looking for things saps the creative process.

Losing things is a sign of disorganization. A book called *The Borrowers* attempts to explain how items just "disappear." This book tells of the little people who live under the floorboards and behind the baseboards of houses and "borrow" things. That's why they disappear.

A lot of these little people used to live at my house. They must not like living in organized houses, however, because since I organized mine they seem to have moved out.

Living in the Clouds

World hunger, dedication to the children and youth of our nation, art, music, literature, careers—these are areas that deserve our time. Dusting, moving a dish from one place to another— how can such things be important in the light of such weighty pursuits? They seem insignificant by comparison.

The trouble is that if we are disorganized at home, we can lose our chance to do something about the problems we consider more important. How can we finish the book we are writing if we can't find the first six chapters of it? How can we organize a drive to ease world hunger if we can't locate the addresses of the people and organizations we need to help us? And we all know the big hindrance of "I'll do wonderful things for the world—just as soon as I get this house under control."

Psychological Hang-Ups

Because Messies are born with a problem when it comes to organization, housekeeping has frequently been a problem from childhood. If Mother is a Cleanie, the situation can be frustrating for both Mother and child. Mother can't understand why the job she gives her child is so poorly done or only half completed.

The child, on the other hand, may think she has done it well, or she may have been distracted by something else and forgotten that the job was not completed.

Mom becomes frustrated and sees this as evidence of an uncooperative spirit. The child may be surprised to learn that the job is poorly done; she cannot understand why Mom is so upset. She becomes resentful at what seems to her to be unjust criticism.

So housekeeping becomes associated with unpleasantness early in life. It is only a short step from here to the idea that housekeeping causes frustration and should be avoided. After all, if you don't try it, you can't fail.

But we've long since left childhood. We can back up, look squarely at the problem as it exists today, and take a new and mature running leap at getting our houses in order. 'Cause I'll tell you this: you haven't seen frustration till you've tried to live in a house that you don't work on.

Depression or Emotional Upset

One of my worst periods of housekeeping was at a time when I was going through a trying emotional experience in another part of my life. I felt as if I were walking in molasses; things just didn't get done. Whatever a person's weakness is, it gets worse during such times. My bad housekeeping became my terrible housekeeping.

I don't believe I would have been able to respond to help in organizing my house during that time, even if help had been given. I had to wait until the psychological problem righted itself before my housekeeping returned to merely "bad."

Frequently, however, the housekeeping actually causes the depression. The feeling of being out of control and the problems caused by poor housekeeping can lead to such despondency that housework is further neglected, and a destructive downward spiral begins.

Sometimes this is accelerated if some overwhelming event occurs. A flood, hurricane, earthquake, or some natural disaster that further messes up the house can easily destroy all hope of ever getting control.

A less traumatic event, such as your mother moving, with her furniture, into your already crowded house; the moving of furnishings from an office that has been closed into your place for storage because there is no other place to keep them; the starting of a home business requiring storage of some items— any of these may bring about the breaking point.

If housekeeping is causing your depression, the only way I know to overcome the downward spiral is by taking control of things. It is not easy to begin; but one success, however small, will lead to another, and slowly a pattern of success will emerge. Remember, it took you a long time to get into this situation, and it will take a while to get out. The important thing is to be heading in the right direction. You are allowed to get discouraged occasionally, but not to give up.

Always remember—you don't have to aim for perfection. You just want to be a successful, average housekeeper.

Selective Neglect

An accomplished young violinist on her way to stardom was asked how she developed her playing to such a high level. "I use a system of selective neglect. I used to do things like chores, errands, and other personal activities first, before practicing, and then begin my practicing. Now, I put practicing first. The other things are deliberately neglected."

Smart thinking. We can't do it all. In this world of so many opportunities, obligations, and choices, we must put our top priorities first and, with good conscience, deliberately neglect a lot of the less important things.

5

There Is a Reason—
It Is Not Laziness

Every why hath a wherefore.

WILLIAM SHAKESPEARE, *COMEDY OF ERRORS*

Messies are generally wonderful people. Just between you and me, I think they are a cut above the average. They are creative, intelligent, nice people. My mother once answered a hundred calls making reservations for a class I was giving. She said it seemed to her that Messies were the nicest people in the world. One of the pleasures of having the class is meeting such interesting folks.

Messies are optimistic. Not many people could keep on going in the face of such discouragement and still hold on to such good humor. Fatigue and frustration take their toll at times, but somehow Messies keep going, looking for a better day.

If Messies are so wonderful, why, then, do they live "that way"? The reason is that housekeeping, though it seems to be

---

Poor Memory: "Why are you late for dinner? Oh, I left you behind at the supermarket—again?"

Distractibility: "I just had that in my hand. Where did it go?"

Disorganized Thinking: "Your briefcase? I put it in a safe place. Well, I must have thought the laundry hamper was safe!" or "I filed the dog's inoculation papers with insurance papers. They both have to do with safety. Sort of."

Visual Tune-Out: "I didn't notice all those things piled on the stairs. How long have those been there?"

Slow Movement: "I know you can set the table in five minutes. You're just going to have to wait if you want me to do it."

---

a natural skill, is really a complex grouping of small, learned skills. If we are weak in one or several of these skills, we can run into all kinds of trouble in housecleaning and never know why. It is like someone who is color-blind but not aware of it trying to make a career as an interior decorator: He or she would be gravely handicapped.

Most Messies are handicapped by these factors. Let's look at them more closely.

Poor Memory

One characteristic common to Messies is absentmindedness. We seem to have difficulty remembering the simplest things. I have a terrible memory, but it used to be worse! I frequently locked myself out of my car. Sometimes I would arrive at an appointment only to discover that I had left an important piece of material behind. Worse, sometimes I forgot the appointment itself! Once I left my purse with our entire life savings in it on a park bench. Another time I left my son at the junior high school where I taught math. I simply went home without him!

But if my memory was bad away from our house, it was equally so at home. It failed me so often that I used to be afraid to put anything in a drawer for fear I would forget where it was, or even that I had ever had it. Bills would pile up as I thought, *I'll get to them as soon as I can. I'll keep them out here so I won't forget.*

Then another item I was afraid to put away would go on top of them, and then . . . Soon there would be another "special" pile with who-knows-what in it beside the other piles of things too important to put away. The bill would be gone for good, or at least removed from the area of my influence.

Sometimes we Messies come to grips with some big cleaning project, organize the thing elaborately and well, and then forget what our organizational plan was. "Where *did* I plan to put these papers?"

"Out of sight, out of mind" is a statement of real truth where I am concerned. I cannot tell you how many times I have let the tub run over because I turned on the water, went off to do something else while it filled, and forgot the whole thing. Fortunately, we don't have wall-to-wall carpeting, wooden floors, or an apartment below us.

Forgetting where I am going, losing my keys, letting the bathtub overflow—are these patterns peculiar only to me? While absentmindedness is not limited to Messies, my guess is that it is more common among us.

Distractibility

Messies tend to be easily distracted. If something grabs our attention, it is as difficult for us to ignore as it is for a cat to ignore a mouse.

We notice a good book and begin reading it while cleaning the bookshelf. We take an item from the drawer or closet we are cleaning to put in a better storage place, but first we have to clear a place for it. Messes spring up like anthills because of our big housecleaning project. Cleaning this way is tiring and messy too.

If a person flits from one job to another—straightening this, clearing that—that's distractibility. Often a job is begun, the phone rings or a child interrupts, and the task is left, or worse, forgotten. An absentminded person usually cannot do two things at one time. Distractibility is akin to absentmindedness.

One of the stories I like best is of the professor who met a student as he crossed the campus. The two stopped to talk. When they finished conversing, the professor asked the student which way he, the professor, had been heading. When the student told him he had been heading toward his office, he replied, "Good, then I have eaten," and continued happily on his way. Now that's distractibility!

Disorganized Thinking

Why are some people more organized than others? Some people are born organized, and some are not . . . or so it seems to me. It may be due to something in the nervous system.

Studies have been done relating right- or left-handedness to organizational ability. The theory is that people who are ambidextrous (who can use either the right or the left hand) tend to be disorganized because the brain gets signals from different sources and has difficulty establishing organizational patterns. A person who is strongly right- or left-handed keeps using the same routes in the nervous system and therefore finds it easier to do the tasks that require organization.

After I graduated from college I did a survey of how people knew their right hands from their left. The typical reply was, "You just know." This was not too useful to me because I didn't "just know." If, therefore, you are not quick to tell one hand from another, you might be consoled—a little—to know that your inability to organize is not so much your fault as your nervous system's. It is good for batters in baseball and for sculptors to be ambidextrous—but it is bad for organizers.

Beyond the ambidextrous possibility is a mysterious inability Messies have about putting things in order. We tend to see each item as unique in itself and find it hard to group with other items. We also tune in to many characteristics of the items we are organizing, not just the main ones, and therefore can see many different possible ways of organizing them. All of this intellectual overdoing makes it difficult for us to categorize things. Categorizing is the backbone of organized thinking.

Marty will come to the end of her patience with the disorganization in her house and say, "I've just got to get these things organized." She moves clutter from off her dresser and puts it on the bed to be worked on. Then the process stops. She doesn't know where to go from there. She is lucky if she ever gets the clutter off the bed and back onto the dresser where it can wait for another "reorganization."

Visual Tune-Out

Visual tune-out has nothing to do with being unable to see. It does have to do with having what you see register. Some of us are not very quick on the visual uptake. When my family passes an accident scene, my husband and children see many more details than I do: "Did you notice the woman in the front seat of the blue car and the woman and little boy beside the station wagon?"

I am doing well if I notice the cars. Given enough time, I would pick out the details, but it doesn't come quickly or easily as we drive by.

Now apply this idea of visual sensitivity to housekeeping. Cleanies are visually alert. They want to see clear, clean, uncluttered lines. If they finish a cup of coffee and don't want another one, the cup is gone, swooped up to the kitchen and sometimes washed, rinsed, and put away in order to maintain the clean lines of orderliness. A Cleanie friend once told me she wished she could tune out a fluff of thread on the carpet—but she had to pick it up, no matter how tired she was.

A Messie, on the other hand, can tolerate a great deal of clutter simply because she is not sensitive to visual things. An educator would say the difficulty is a lack of response to visual stimuli due to a figure-ground problem. No matter what others call it, when company comes to the door unexpectedly, we call it embarrassed.

Slow Movement

A Messie's slowness usually isn't because of slow muscle movement. Some jobs take a long time to figure out.

Sorting laundry is the worst for me. There are five people in my family. After my eyes send a message to my brain telling me what they see, my brain has to figure out two things: whose piece of clothing it is and which of the piles in front of me belongs to each respective person.

Every piece of clothing requires this process. All that thinking can wear a person out, especially if the piles to be sorted become too large.

However, I have seen folks sort laundry zip, zip, zip—and they don't even seem to be thinking. The point is that if a person processes information slowly he is not going to be able to work as fast as others who do not have the same difficulty, and this can make housekeeping slow and fatiguing.

Sometimes the idea of doing a job perfectly slows a person down. The job has to be so good that as a result, one little corner of the house is clean while the rest is still cluttered.

If you have one of these problems or all of them, can you still hope to take charge of your house and your time? Yes, you can! I know, because I have done it.

6

Reasons for the Reason

*If I change my thinking, I will
change my feelings.
If I change my feelings, I will
change my actions.
If I change my actions, I will change my life.*

When I first woke up to the fact that I was not the only person who struggled with messiness and started getting together with other folks like me to find help, I was amazed at how much alike our problems were. Many similarities have already been mentioned in earlier chapters. As a matter of fact, you may be asking yourself if I have been looking into your windows, or into your brain. *How did she know all this stuff?* you ask yourself.

I know it because I saw these ideas, feelings, and habits in myself. I know it because Messies in small groups and personal conversations confirmed that they were "different" from more organized people in the same way I was. I know it because groups of Messies I spoke to laughed the laugh of recognition when I mentioned our peculiar ways of thinking.

The characteristics that get us into trouble are not bad character traits. Many are good ones. The problem is that we overdo or misapply them. Most people value the past, but we overvalue it and keep way too much. Most people want to make good decisions, but we fear making an error to the extent that we are afraid to make any decision, and organizing stalls because of it. Other people forget things now and again, but we forget so much that we are afraid to put things out of our sight. Other people misplace things every once in a while, but we do it as a way of life.

I have gained new insights over the years. In addition, in recent years, researchers and other professionals have begun to look into the problems of disorganization. Some of their discoveries confirm what we guessed years ago. Some add interesting new dimensions to the problem.

Obsessive Compulsive Disorder (OCD)

People who research the area of "collecting" classify hoarding as one of the anxiety disorders known as obsessive compulsive disorder (OCD). Sometimes it's a relief to find that it has a name. Sometimes it's scary or annoying to have a psychological name for such a mundane thing as just keeping too much stuff. Obviously, some people who keep too much stuff won't ever be diagnosed with OCD. Nonetheless, they have enough of the characteristics of the problem to benefit from what the researchers find out about it.

Messies keep things for three reasons.

1. *We save for the past.* We love the past. No, we overlove it. It is part of us. Items from the past (even old receipts) are

like a moment from our lives that has been crystallized. To get rid of anything from the past feels like getting rid of part of ourselves. If the items belonged to beloved relatives or friends, then we feel like we are rejecting or dishonoring them if we let the things go. It feels as though they are somehow mixed in their belongings.

Because we are not able to remember with the perfectionistic clarity we think the past deserves, we keep these things (often sitting out) as reminders. What good does it do to have lived if our thoughts and actions are not conserved in memory or concrete form? These bits and pieces of stuff prove that we have lived full lives.

Because of the passion with which we regard these belongings, it hurts us even to think about discarding them.

2. *We save for the future.* Everybody wants to make reasonable preparation for future needs. Being perfectionists, we want to make preparation for any possible need that may be known to man or beast, real or imagined (and we have great imaginations). Nobody can foretell the future. Anything might be needed in the future. Period costumes for a play, an ostrich feather for a science display, old catalog pictures for a history paper, candles galore in case the electricity goes off for a long time—you name it and we can think of a good reason we need to keep it "just in case." We also save things we have no earthly use for because we know that if we keep them long enough, we'll think of something. Making multiple use of things (bleach bottles for holding clothespins, soda bottles for planters, stocking toes stuffed with soap slivers for a soap-on-the-rope substitute) is also common for us.

A lot of fear lurks in the background of our decision making. Nobody has yet figured out what awful thing will happen if we should get rid of something we will need later. The only thing we know for sure is that if we or anybody else needed something and we had not saved it (gasp!), we would feel really, *really, REALLY* bad. In order to avoid that possibility, we keep it.

Organized people who don't feel compelled to oversave for the future would say, "Oh, well, I got rid of that old thing long ago," and not give it another thought. But not us; we are responsible people who will try to be ready—for anything at all!

3. *We save to define ourselves with our possessions.* Holding on to exercise clothes we haven't used in years confirms that we are dedicated to fitness. Clothes in a smaller size announce our intention to lose weight. Keeping moth-eaten sewing material and out-of-fashion patterns proves we are seamstresses, and displaying never-used cooking utensils is evidence that we are cooks.

Those special holiday magazines; newspaper clippings or newspapers waiting to be clipped; books we have read, partly read, or never read—all indicate our various interests. Old musical instruments, dried-up paints, jumbled craft materials, old flower bulbs, and all sorts of other creative junk shout that we are vitally creative people.

Messies who define themselves in this way feel they must overdo in order to prove they are important. All of these items are evidence of such efforts.

The problem, of course, is that none of this works. Trying to keep all of this stuff just makes things worse because we can't handle the overload of belongings. We keep things from the past and then can't find our wedding photo album to show our children. We have boxes and boxes of Band-Aids somewhere, but when our child cuts his knee, we have to use toilet paper and Scotch tape.

The things we keep to define ourselves mock us on a daily basis because we are just too cluttered and too disorganized to do any of the good things they stand for.

Giving a name to a problem is important. But the most important thing is to get the help we need to loosen the grip of keeping more stuff than we can handle. If you want more information about trying to break the "collecting" habit yourself, get my twenty-four-page booklet, *I've Got to Get Rid of This Stuff: Strategies for Overcoming Hoarding (The Packrat Syndrome)*. (See p. 264–65 for ordering information.)

If you want more information from a professional standpoint, contact one of the foundations for OCD. Your library or the internet can give you up-to-date information on how to do that.

Attention Deficit Disorder (ADD)

When my book *Messie No More* hit the market, no chapter got more interest than the chapter on attention deficit disorder (ADD, or ADHD). Since that time people have become aware that ADD is not limited to hyperactive school-age boys. ADD is now being diagnosed in adults who may or may not be hyperactive.

One group of special interest to us is adult women who are being diagnosed with ADD. In adulthood its chief characteristic is distractibility, and one of the chief evidences of this distractibility is disorganization.

According to Dale Jordan in *Attention Deficit Disorder*, disorganization is the "earmark of adult Attention Deficit Disorder." In his excellent book *ADD Success Stories*, Thom Hartman states, "People with ADD are often disorganized and cluttered, and can benefit tremendously from learning organizational strategies that teach them how to impose order and systems on their schooling or work."

In their classic book *Driven to Distraction*, Hollowell and Ratey mention several characteristics of adult ADD. Some that relate to causes of messiness are an intolerance of boredom, a sense of insecurity, a tendency to be creative, a tendency to have many simultaneous projects, and an inaccurate perception of self.

In her book *Women with Attention Deficit Disorder*, Sari Solden states that "disorganization in one form or another is the subject that most women with ADD talk about the most in counseling."

Some of the organizational problems a person with ADD is likely to experience and that may help in diagnosing ADD are:

- Starting a craft project or decorating job and not completing it, leaving behind a half-done job.
- Putting something down and not paying attention to where it is. Consequently, it is lost.
- Moving things and forgetting where it was put because attention was not focused while doing it.
- Developing a complex organizational system and forgetting what the system was. Or continually changing systems.
- Not having an organizational intuition; just putting things away in a place that seems good at that moment.
- Making "stupid" mistakes like putting in baking soda instead of baking powder or putting the wrong type of film in the camera.
- Lateness and confusion about where the time has gone.
- Not noticing things that are sitting out.
- Inability to judge how long a task is going to take.
- Not following through with activities: opening and then failing to close closet doors and drawers, washing the laundry and even folding it but then failing to put it away.

Overlapping of OCD and ADD Characteristics

We must look at and make arrangements to handle the characteristics over which we do not have as much control. Although
there are many distinctives, you may have noticed that some of
these characteristics of ADD are similar to the characteristics
of OCD. Some of the overlapping areas are:

Poor memory. Research suggests a memory weakness in folks
with OCD as well as ADD. In his book *Do You Have Attention Disorder?* James Lawrence Thomas states, "People
who don't have attention deficit disorder often cannot believe that a person could forget so much and so quickly. . . .
It seems that the part of their brain that is supposed to
remember just doesn't work very well for some ADD
adults."

Organizational inability. In his research on OCD, Frost men-
tions an inability to categorize that causes difficulty in
basic organizing skills. In their book Answers to Distraction Hollowell and Ratey state that "the ADD brain lacks
the internal organization that naturally leads most people
to structure their lives."

Distractibility. Leaving books out and going from project
to project in a distracted way is certainly classic ADD
behavior, as Frost observes in his "Cognitive Behavioral
Model" research paper.

Decision making. Like a person with OCD, a person who
has ADD may hesitate to begin a decision-making project such as disposing of possessions. She knows from
experience that when attention fluctuates, she may make
a poor or hasty decision.

Commenting on her observations about the similarities, Sari Solden suggests that "a person with ADD may develop compensations which look like compulsions or obsessions as a way of coping with the problems of ADD."

The overlapping of these characteristics is interesting to us who struggle with them on a daily basis. Once they come out of the dark, they are not as puzzling. Knowing that they are common helps us to focus on exactly the characteristics we must overcome if we are to be organized.

If we spend too much time on the psychological causes of this thing as seen by doctors and researchers, we could get bogged down in concern, self-pity, despair, or whatever. Don't go there. If knowing about ADD or OCD is helpful, use that knowledge. If it is not, discard it and move on.

Areas for Change

Go slowly, pace yourself, and prepare for a long-range change, instituting a little at a time. Just keep going until you have made the changes you need to make. Consider the following areas for change:

- *Toughness.* We have come to value our tough "I can take it" attitude. Up until now we have had to have that attitude to face the daily insults that our way of life has hurled our way. It has been a good protection. But now we need to move away from that to the softer attitude of "I will take better care of myself."

- *Drama.* Up until now we have struggled daily with clutter and confusion. We have grown used to the drama of the fight. It tests our ingenuity. Sometimes we get an

61

adrenaline rush when we solve an organizational crisis. We may miss the excitement of the struggle. We have to be willing to live with less excitement.

- *Perfectionism.* We will need to loosen the grip of that compulsion to "do it right or not at all." Perfectionism is a strong roadblock to moving forward for folks with ADD. Adopt the attitude, "If it's worth doing at all, it is worth doing wrong." That should challenge some of the perfectionism!

- *Frugality.* Many of us adhere to the "Waste not, want not" outlook. But this knee-jerk attitude toward getting rid of things makes us want to keep too much. Some naturally organized people can indulge frugality. Those of us with problems can't. We end up with more stuff than even the most organized person could handle and we wonder why we are so disorganized. Half of our organizational problems would be solved if we had half the stuff we do.

- *Creativity.* We can happily accept that most people with ADD have a strongly creative side. We can think of more projects than any one person could ever do in one lifetime. We can think of more uses for objects than is practical. Sometimes we keep stuff we can't think of any use for just because we know that, given enough time, we will think of some use for it. Creative people have to have more things in their lives than less creative folks, but this has to be controlled or it will get out of hand. Then truly productive creativity will be hindered.

- *Sentimentality.* Taken to an extreme, sentimentality causes messes. We cannot keep every item that gives us a warm feeling about the past. That will crush our present and our future. For the sake of order in our lives, we need to be selective and willing to let some of those heartwarming memorabilia go.

- *Power.* Because we sense deep down inside the power that some of the characteristics of ADD give to us and the power of our intelligence, we think we can do more than we can. It is true that most ADD folks have a certain characteristic energy and drive that enables them to do a lot. But it is often unfocused and misused. We try to do too much, not recognizing the limits of time, energy, and attention. We need to be willing to attempt less but with more focus. Perhaps this is what Hollowell and Ratey meant by the characteristic "inaccurate perception of self."

What I am suggesting is not a small matter. To make changes in our lives at this very basic level of our personality challenges our long-held view of who we are. Many of these ideas and feelings have their roots deep in our family histories, in our personal histories, and even in our values. It is scary and painful to change in this way, but it is scary and painful to keep on living with pernicious disorganization, too.

Insight can come quickly, but changing basic thought and emotional patterns must come more slowly. Later you will read about organizational tips and techniques for organizing. These are great. But they work only when they are built on the internal reorganization of thinking and feeling. The bottom line is, are you willing to leave a crazy, unmanageable, and disorganized lifestyle for a more orderly and serene lifestyle? Don't worry about how you can accomplish it right now. If you are willing, you are already well on your way.

It's a Tough World Out There

Outside our houses lurk stress, pressure, and sometimes danger we can't always control. We can control the atmosphere inside our homes. One of the most compelling reasons for developing a calm atmosphere in our homes is to create a haven for recovery and strengthening.

What a shame if the most stressful place in our lives is our messy house. As William James, the noted psychologist, said, "Nothing is so fatiguing as the eternal hanging on of uncompleted tasks." Disorder robs us of the pleasure and comfort we want our house to provide for us.

Let's reevaluate. How important is the condition of the house? Important enough to put first in our priorities and continue to put first until the atmosphere strengthens our tired bones and soothes our fatigued souls.

PART 2

Turning Things Around

7

Developing Organizing Attitudes

*Attitude determines our dreams and
goals. Persistence gets us there.*

Make-It-Easy-on-Yourself Principles

You can learn organizational strategies that make sense and will
work for you. In *ADD Success Stories* Thom Hartman states,
"People with ADD . . . can benefit tremendously from learning
organizational strategies that teach them how to impose order
and systems on their schooling or work." Everyone can benefit
from this approach. Here are some of those strategies.

If It Is Easy, It Will Be Faster

If it is faster, you are more likely to do it. One of the problems
with accomplishing a task is that ideas flit quickly in and out of
focus in the brain. If a job is hard to start, it is difficult to maintain
attention to start it. Complex systems are roadblocks. Use the
K.I.S.S. method (Keep It Super Simple). Because we are often

very intellectually oriented, we can think up systems that are too complicated to use.

Unclutter Your Life

Having too many things is time-consuming, distracting, and frustrating to handle. Get rid of the excess.

Simplify Your Life in Other Ways

In her national bestselling books on simplicity of life, Elaine St. James suggests we disentangle ourselves from a number of the modern "efficiency" devices that were supposed to improve our lives but end up complicating them. In her book *Simplify Your Life*, she suggests and justifies wearing clothes longer between washings, dropping call waiting, simplifying your wardrobe, simplifying your eating habits, spending a day a month in solitude, taking a retreat once a year, and the like.

H. Norman Wright includes Christian principles in his excellent book *Simplify Your Life and Get More Out of It!* He leads his reader step-by-step into a saner lifestyle.

My book *The Messie Motivator* appeals to the Messie to build conscious serenity into life, to find satisfaction apart from things and activities.

Follow the 80/20 Rule

Pareto, an Italian economist, discovered a rule relating to economy that has since been applied in many areas. In time management, simply put, it is this: Only 20 percent of the tasks before us will be productive; 80 percent will not.

Actually the rule is more specific. Twenty percent of the tasks will result in 80 percent of the accomplishments while the other 80 percent of the tasks will result in only 20 percent of the accomplishments. I like the first and less complex way of stating it. Either way, you get the idea.

Find the important 20 percent and concentrate on those tasks. The only way to identify the 20 percent is by taking quiet, private time at the beginning of the day to review, reflect upon, and prioritize your schedule.

Make Incremental but Permanent Changes

In their program on managing projects, priorities, and deadlines, Jonathan and Susan Clark state: "Small changes, over time, can make a big difference." Anthony Robbins uses the acronym of CANEI to remind himself to seek Constant And Never Ending Improvement in incremental steps. You don't have to do everything at once. Just determine the direction you want to go, make the significant small changes to start, and keep going in that direction. Remember, the 80/20 rule tells us that if we make a 20 percent change in the right areas, we can expect an 80 percent change in our lives.

Take Breaks When Things Get Spacey

Distractibility comes in episodes, triggered by stress or other factors. When one of these spaced-out times comes, stop, take a break, have a cup of tea in a quiet place if possible, and breathe deeply before you go back to the task that got out of hand to begin with.

Take Time to Refuel Your Spirit

Spend time alone at a park, the beach, a retreat house, or wherever. Make it an all-day thing or an overnighter. Or maybe even longer. You need time to reflect, enjoy nature, unwind, and recharge. I try to get away alone for a day or two every year, usually around the first of the year, to set goals and priorities for myself.

Join a Support Group

There are ADD support groups and Messies Anonymous support groups in many parts of the country. Most of the internet servers have online chat rooms and support groups. Seek out those who share your concerns. Messies Anonymous has a website that has several active online support groups: www.messies.com.

Use Organizing Books

Peruse the library or bookstore until you find one of the excellent books on organizing that speaks to your organizational needs and style.

Read Books on ADD

Several books on ADD have sections on organizing, but your biggest help will be to educate yourself about the problem if you feel it may apply to you. One of the possibilities you will want to consider is medication.

My book called *Why Can't I Get Organized? Success Strategies for Those with Attention Deficit Disorder and Other Distractible Folks* (available from Messies Anonymous) concentrates on the issue of how ADD affects organizing and what can be done about it.

Get "Another Pair of Eyes"

When we have lived with clutter for a long time we fail to see it impartially. Sometimes we fail to see it at all. Frequently all it takes is someone from the outside to say, "Do you use these hydroponic boxes on the front porch anymore?" for you to tune in to the fact that they are ugly and unnecessary and for you to get rid of them.

Fear of Changing

Maybe you are saying to yourself, "I am a little afraid to change." Great! This feeling shows that you are really understanding the situation and that you are seriously considering changing. You have good reasons to fear making change. It is a good thing to look at those reasons before we go any farther so that we can face them and begin to get them out of the way of progress.

There are a lot of reasons why those of us who are chronically disorganized (Messies) fear letting go of disorganization.

- *Fear of forgetting.* The objects we want to keep are our pasts frozen in solid form.
- *Fear of losing ourselves.* We mix ourselves in some fashion with our belongings because we do not observe personal boundaries as much as others.
- *Fear of losing our distinctive personalities.* Impulsiveness, overdoing, creativity, and disorganization are so much a part of us that we worry what we would be like if these qualities were modified or eliminated.
- *Fear of extremism.* Knowing our weakness for overdoing, we are afraid we will go overboard and be compulsively neat or clean.
- *Fear of hurting our belongings.* We assign them some kind of personification (similar to the way men name their cars, etc.) and want them to find a good home.

- *Fear of losing others who we imagine live on in some small fashion in the belongings they owned.* This is especially true of belongings of those who have died.
- *Fear of having to face reality.* As long as we are distracted by this problem, we can ignore other problems we really don't want to face.
- *Fear of boredom.* The daily struggle with clutter offers a certain excitement and adrenaline rush we would miss if the drama of the problem were gone. We fear serenity. In actuality, it does take a while to get used to.
- *Fear of power.* If we can get control of our belongings, then we may feel responsible to be mature in other areas as well. It is easier to be a victim.
- *Fear of relationship changes.* Some relationships revolve around our messiness. If we lose our messiness, our relationships will be jarred.
- *Fear we will not have our needs met.* A lot of stuff we keep is for the unknown and scary future. If we get rid of it, will we be cared for in the future?
- *Fear of not helping others who might need some of these belongings.*
- *Fear of not being able to find something if we keep only one of it.* If we have five bottles of furniture glue, our chances of finding one of them is five times greater than if we keep only one (or so we think).
- *Fear of making the wrong decision.* Messies are perfectionists. Suppose we get rid of something we really will need later? We are afraid not to be perfect.

Don't let fear hold you back from the wonderful way of life you know is available for you. You will be surprised at who you can become when you are willing to face the fear and do it anyway.

Attitudes for Success

Failure is seldom caused by a major catastrophe. It is a series of little failures. Success is the same.

Knowing about the characteristics that have been holding us back can be liberating at first. We have an "Ah-ha! So that's the problem!" experience. But lingering on the problems can be downright discouraging.

Let's not do that to ourselves. Put those hindrances behind you and turn your attention to what you need to do to get on that wonderful road to a well-run life and house.

Hold On to Hope

Many who have lived with disorganization for a long time have ceased to hope for a more successful life. They have been disappointed so many times that they are afraid to think that there can be relief. But deep down smolders one small ember of hope. The truth is that life can change. We can have the beauty and order we long for. We can have not only hope but also success. Don't give up!

Practice Self-Care

Messiness is a disease of self-neglect. There comes a time when, no matter how hard it is to change, we are so sick and tired of living with the mess and the chaos it causes in our lives that we are willing to do whatever is necessary to change. The problem of chronic, day-after-day disorganization is not to be taken lightly. Living a disorganized life causes a lot of stress. Stress may lead to illnesses, depression, and worse. We hurt ourselves when we live a life in which we:

- can't find items we need (like car keys, a belt, socks, etc. when we are already running late)
- have an unpleasant-looking house because of the clutter
- are afraid we will be called upon to produce papers and can't locate them (as for the IRS, insurance company, receipts)
- have to go through piles again and again in order to re-trieve papers
- fall behind on our tasks (paying bills, getting out reports, etc.)
- isolate ourselves out of embarrassment about the house
- always have to reinvent where to put something or how to do something because we lack a system
- experience poor self-esteem because we lack control over our environment
- participate in repeated arguments about the condition of the house

Being disorganized is very painful. We can change. We need to take the mature route and start being responsible for taking better care of ourselves. At its most basic level, this means get-ting rid of the burden of the clutter.

Encourage Self-Confidence

Now that we have some understanding of the problem and have started to get some help, we look around and see that others in our condition have gotten their organizational act together.

If they can do it, we can too. Think, *I'm not lazy, stupid, or crazy. Somehow, some way, I can do it!* Avoid the victim mentality. Take charge of your life. Disorganization is just one factor in a complex life filled with many challenges. It does not override every other consideration.

Seek Passion

Over the long haul, just learning organizational systems will not be enough for most people. Somewhere along the line we have got to catch a vision of the beauty we can build into our lives. We need to feel passionately the love of the environment we can create.

Sometimes people give up organizing simply because there is nothing important enough to them to keep working. Seek beauty and order with gusto!

Ask for Help

Shame and stoic self-reliance have kept us isolated with our problem. It may be that one of the smartest things we can do for ourselves is to get outside help either from family, friends, a self-help group, professional organizers (see "Resources" for further information), or some other wonderful person who may come into our lives. You are the only one who can say when you are ready to get outside help. Don't rule it out. There are some organizational tasks we will never be able to do on our own because we lack the innate talent. Outside help can be a significant contribution to ordering our world.

Delegate

Delegating may mean not doing everything in the house yourself. You may make a list of jobs for the family. (Getting the family to help is a whole subject in itself and is not easily done. Look into my *When You Live with a Messie* and many of the books on child raising for tips.) Don't think you need to do everything yourself (wrap gifts, bake turkey, etc.). Find ways either to get volunteers or to hire help in order to delegate the doing of things you are not good at or don't have time for.

Be Willing to Make Adjustments

Give yourself permission to do things differently if that is what it takes to meet your own peculiar organizational needs.

Make adjustments in your standards. This may mean lowering your ideal standards to more reasonable levels. This is no time to hold to perfectionism and the "Do it right or not at all" approach. Cut yourself some slack.

Make adjustments in your activities. Be willing to set the buzzer on the kitchen clock when you put water on to boil so the pot won't burn. Be willing to make any of the other specific adjustments suggested later on that will meet your needs. Don't tell yourself that intelligent people don't need these kinds of mental props. A lot of us who are very intelligent are smart enough to know that these things will make our lives better.

Seek Serenity

Serenity is very hard to get used to when you have been living with chaos and the adrenaline high that the struggle has caused. Many Messies seek out exciting, high stimulation activities, probably because such activities help them to focus themselves. At first order, beauty, and harmony in life and home seem uncomfortable. After we adjust to it, serenity feels wonderful! But it does take time to adjust. Be willing to experience serenity.

Use meditation, devotional and inspirational reading, and tapes such as the Messies Anonymous tape "Create Your Dream and Live It." There is a world of help available to you in libraries, bookstores, and through catalogs. Take advantage of it.

Value Your Differences

Messies have some characteristics that make them very special and valuable people indeed. Don't discount the creativity, the curiosity, the intelligence that is a part of your Messie heritage.

Go with the Flow of Your Own Personality

Although you can learn some organizational tips from an organized person, copying exactly her style will not likely be in your best interest. For example, you can expect to need to have more items around you than many of your more naturally organized friends. This may include having more books, magazines, clothes, and food in the refrigerator. Although you need to accept that fact about yourself, you must not allow more excess than you can keep organized. In other words, you must be in control of yourself.

Honor Your Need to Create

You need to maintain the best balance possible for good mental health in your life. If you have a creative spirit, that means you must create to be happy. Perhaps it will be poetry, art, writing, or music. It may be crafts, sewing, baking, refinishing furniture, or several of these and some other things. Be sure to make time to express yourself in that way. If you neglect that aspect of your personality, without your realizing what has happened, a certain kind of malaise will set in and make it difficult for you to do other things right.

Since the act of creating is often a disorganized affair, control what you do by doing only one activity at a time. Plan ahead as to how you will store things and get storage supplies. Put things up when you finish using them for that session of creativity, even though that means that you will have to get them out the next time you use them.

Be Cheerful

Living with the struggle to organize can be very discouraging. You have dealt with it for a very long time and have kept up your courage in a remarkable way. Sometimes you may be very disheartened. Once you realize that there is a cause and that a cure is possible, you may resent the lost years and opportunities of the past. Perhaps you will become angry that this has happened to you. Your self-esteem may still be low and, of course, there is the mess to deal with. There is a place for all of these feelings. But don't take them too far. Work with your feelings. Work through them. Then let that resilience that has gotten you this far strengthen you for the change ahead. When you step back and look at things objectively, you have a lot to be cheerful about.

Forgive Yourself Quickly

When you falter, and you will, keep going without self-recriminations. Try not to waste too much energy on shame and discouragement. When you have done your best and some "stupid" thing blindsides you unexpectedly, say to yourself, "I guess it's my clutter tendency kicking in again."

If possible, seek comfort from an understanding friend. Expect and prepare mentally for failures along the way. Your progress will not be as fast or as consistent as you may wish. You will never be perfect. That's okay. Just keep going in the right direction.

Accept Your Weaknesses

They are there and they will never go away entirely. The sooner you are comfortable with that fact, the less power they will have over you. Be smart when it comes to knowing your own weaknesses.

Your disorganization is not the only aspect of your life. You are a complex combination of strengths and weaknesses playing off each other in a multifaceted social world.

Get Rid of a Make-Do Mentality

Don't be satisfied with just whatever comes your way. You are too important, your life is too important, to go that route. Honor the fact of your significance. Treat yourself with respect by insisting on a well-run life.

Dream Bigger Dreams for Yourself

Strive for excellence. You are on earth for a purpose. Disorganization can keep you from that purpose. It can beat you down and keep your eyes lowered from what you really can be and do. It is as you step out of the hold that disorder has on you that you can lift your eyes to what you can become.

Some people don't bother to organize because they don't have a reason important enough to bother doing it. There is a wonder and wildness to life. Don't miss living it to the full.

The Bigger Picture

Growing away from overscheduling, perfectionism, and self-neglect is not entirely a personal matter. We are unique, valuable people. God put you here for a purpose. There is an orderly and effective individual within us. Our contribution to the world is being warped and dissipated by the clutter that hinders our full expression of our abilities. The world is waiting to be ennobled by our fullest participation.

It is said that someone asked Michelangelo how he was able to carve the magnificent statue of David from a block of marble. "David was always in the marble," he replied. "I just chipped away the parts of the stone that were not David."

Chip the debris out of your life. You may be surprised at the wonderful person hidden there.

8

Cleanies I Have Known

*These I have loved: white plates
and cups, clean—gleaming.*

RUPERT BROOKE

Unlike Messies, Cleanies have mental schedules they themselves are not aware of. Their minds are like computers going down their list of things to do.

The power that activates the computer is in the eyes. Again and again they say, "When I see . . ." or "If it looks dirty, I . . ."

Their goals are visual and they become uncomfortable if something is out of place. Cleanies are not afraid to use short-cuts because they are confident in their own cleaning ability and don't feel it necessary to prove anything by doing things the hard way.

They tend to get up with a bang and get going with purpose. They frequently have a time goal in mind and work fast to meet it. You might think they are uptight people. They don't seem to be. In fact, they often are gracious, warm, and creative. They can afford to be because they have enough time to do whatever they want to do!

These are general statements, of course. Let's meet some of these paragons individually, to see if we can learn to do as they do.

One thing my Cleanie friends have in common is that they don't understand. They don't understand at all. I can always tell true Cleanies by the way they react when they hear that I teach a class on housekeeping. They look blank—very blank.

"Oh, it is a class on cooking."

"No, housekeeping."

"Oh, I see, a class on interior decorating."

"No, actually it's *housekeeping*."

"Oh."

Silence. How can you continue discussing the inconceivable? Why would anybody need a class on housekeeping?

One blank-faced woman told me soberly that if I did have a class on housekeeping nobody would come. Since I had been having well-attended classes, I asked her why she thought nobody would come.

"Obviously, if people have messy houses it is because they want them that way. And, if they want them that way, why would they attend the class? So nobody will come."

If Cleanies only knew how we struggle! But housekeeping comes so naturally to them that they don't understand at all.

It follows that the best way to learn from Cleanies is to meet some of them and watch them in action. That is precisely what we are going to do now.

Carmen

Carmen works full-time in the import-export business. She is a widow and has an eleven-year-old daughter.

Going to her small condominium is refreshing. It is beige in color for warmth, but shining and cool to the touch. She has a floor of Italian tile and a lot of glass on tables and shelves. Vertical blinds regulate the light.

She herself radiates style. Most of her wardrobe is beige and black so that she can mix and match freely. Accent colors bring variety to her look.

Carmen has developed several tricks to keep her house beautiful without working at it. She freely admits that she dislikes housework and has better things to do. So she plans not to do it.

When her husband was alive, he used to put the white pillows from the couch on the floor to watch TV. When she bought a new couch, she bought one with attached pillows so that she would not even have to say anything to him about not putting the pillows on the floor.

Carmen also had a countertop that stuck out beyond the wall dividing the living room and kitchen. It fairly begged people to stick something on it as they passed. So they obliged.

Carmen didn't want to have to hassle people about this, so she had her husband extend the wall so the counter was not exposed and tempting. When she bought shelves for her living room, she bought the kind with glass in front so she would not have to dust as frequently.

Since Carmen's condominium is small, she does not have a dirty clothes hamper. Instead, she folds dirty clothes and puts them in a decorative chest at the foot of her bed.

Carmen uses "little minutes." She never cleans cabinets. When the cabinets are nearly empty, she wipes them out. When the refrigerator is nearly empty, she gives it a quick cleaning. When she puts her clean, folded laundry into the drawer, she gives the drawer a quick straightening. So there is no need for a cleaning marathon. She is finished and ready to go at 9:00 or 9:30—a.m. that is!

Joyce

Joyce is a former 10. She used to pull her refrigerator out from the wall weekly and clean behind it. Now she is more relaxed and cruises at a comfortable 8 or 9. Joyce, an artist, is also a collector of trinkets. I do not recommend the trinkets. They are nothing but trouble when it comes to cleaning.

Joyce is married and has an eight-year-old boy, a longhaired dog, and two cats. She works at home full-time as a wife and mother.

If you ask Joyce whether she has a schedule she will say, "No," and then add, "but of course, I do the kitchen floor on Mondays. I don't have to, but I usually do. And I change sheets on Fridays." And on and on it goes.

Joyce keeps a more casual schedule than Carmen and is finished about noon. When I say finished, I mean finished!

Then she is ready for painting. So she paints for a while, watches television, puts away the paints, cooks dinner, and welcomes her family home. It sounds so easy, doesn't it? But I remember days of full-time homemaking when I had the same amount of time and *never* finished.

How does she do it? The key can be found if we listen to what Joyce says: "When I *see* dog hairs, I go over the floor with a dust mop." "I put the paints away because I don't like to *see* them left out. It looks cluttered." "I think it *looks* nicer when the clothes are all put away." Cleanies are very visually oriented and want the house to look pleasant.

Joyce also uses little minutes shining the bathroom mirror with a dry bath towel each day after she brushes her teeth.

Marcella

Marcella is married, has two children, ages six years and five months, and babysits for a one-year-old. She also has a short-haired dog.

Marcella has a lot of trouble telling what schedule she keeps. One thing she does know, she is usually finished by 9:00 or 9:30 a.m.

Her main principle is to keep her house in order so that she never has to do a big cleaning job. She gets up at 5:30 or 6:00 a.m. to feed the baby. She gets her six-year-old, Ginny, up at 7:00 a.m. to leave for school at 8:00.

Ginny is ready by 7:30 and plays with the baby until 8:00. Then the baby is ready for a nap, and Ginny is ready to go to school. From 7:30 to 9:00 or 9:30, Marcella does all of her cleaning.

At 7:30 she cleans the kitchen, does the dishes (no dishwasher), vacuums and mops the kitchen floor, and wipes the counter. Then she makes the two beds (five minutes), wipes down the bathroom (ten minutes), and does a few other chores.

Tuesday and Thursday are her free days, when she is finished by 8:00 or 8:30. Monday and Friday are heavy days, when she works until 9:30, because they are at the beginning and end of the week. Wednesday is a moderate day, when she does a little catching up for the middle of the week.

What does she do on heavy days? She vacuums two bedrooms, one bath, and the den, then dusts the furniture and goes over it with window cleaner. Every day while she does the cleaning, she puts in two loads of laundry to wash, dry, and fold so that everything is done at the same time, and she doesn't have to worry about housecleaning for the rest of the day. She wants to be free for whatever comes up, whether it be business or pleasure.

How does she maintain the house during the day? She puts things away at once.

What does she do the rest of the day? She visits with friends who have children so the children can play together, goes to a painting class, and cares for personal needs such as nails and hair washing.

Of course, Cleanies' tricks of organization don't come naturally to us Messies—that's our problem. Nevertheless, with some thought, we can develop some of the devices that will help us keep our homes as orderly as those of our Cleanie friends. (Well, nearly!)

The truth is we will never become Cleanies. We just would not be comfortable with a level of organization that high. But a larger truth is this: we really do need to upgrade the way we live because we sure aren't comfortable with the way it is now. And we want, desperately want, to change. After my interviews with my Cleanie friends, I discovered another group of housekeepers I call Successful Average Housekeepers. This is a group that does not take housekeeping nearly as seriously as the Cleanies

---

When Housework Isn't Housework

Attitude is everything. How you feel about things is shown by the words you use. Changing the way you think can influence your behavior permanently.

- Housework is really the privilege of managing your home.
- Cleaning your room is actually treating yourself with dignity.
- Organizing is relieving the stress of chaos.
- Keeping things picked up is embracing harmony in your life.
- Making the kids keep things organized is training them for responsible adulthood.

---

and does not work at it with as much discipline as they do. Nonetheless, their homes are always neat enough. They are not suffering from clutter overload because they know a few basic organizational principles and consistently apply them. The result: a consistently okay house.

Now, there's a goal to shoot for. We can do it by finding out what those few basic principles are and consistently applying them in a way that makes sense to us. Then we can join the ranks of that group—Successful Average Housekeepers!

> Once upon a midnight dreary,
> There I stood, my eyes all bleary.
> 'Mid coffee cup and Twinkie wrapper—
> How I yearned to be a midnight napper!
> But once upon a morning bright,
> I'd vowed to clean before the night.
> Though ambition fled before the noon,
> I still refused to change my tune.
>
> Once upon a dawn less dreary,
> My whole house shone, spotless and cheery.
> And though no one would know but I,
> I claimed a victory with my sigh . . .
>
> . . . and woke the kids for breakfast.

9

You Don't Really Want to Be a 10

Nothing in excess.

EURIPIDES

Extremes are always bad. Once in a while you hear about people like the Colyer brothers in New York who were found dead in their home because some trash had fallen on them as they walked through the passageways left by their walls of junk. Such a person is a 0 on the Cleanie scale. No 0s would come to a Messies Anonymous seminar or read this book.

Once, when Messies Anonymous had just begun, we had a ½ come to the seminar. He had disposed of his kitchen appliances so he would have room for more items. He had shelves lining his walls and set up in the middle of his rooms, library style. They held all of his many collections.

He subscribed to thirty-eight magazines a month and kept them all, envisioning the value of a complete collection. He was now starting to store some things outside.

The reason he came to the seminar was to see if we knew of any way to store more things in his, by now, decidedly limited area. Coming to our seminar for this reason is like going to Weight Watchers to inquire if anybody knows where bigger clothing can be bought.

The odd thing was that I felt upset that evening, not because of John—he could live however he wanted—but because his story stirred up in me the desire to have thirty-eight magazine subscriptions and a room full of shelves. That is a scary and uncomfortable feeling. I know how much harm indiscriminate gathering can cause.

The feeling went away by the next day. I wonder if I would feel the same discomfort now that I have broken the gathering habit.

But if a 0 (or ½) is an extreme, so is a 10. When I was a child, we lived in Memphis, Tennessee, where it gets cold in the winter. From time to time I would hear the children of a neighbor begging to come in out of the cold, but their mother wouldn't let them in. When I asked my mother why, she told me the neighbor didn't want her children messing up the house. When we went

---

Messies Focus on the Noble Life

It would be easy to take the approach that Messies lack a certain nobility in their lives, that they do not have an understanding of graciousness. It is tempting to suggest that if Messies would only tune in to the possibilities of charm and beauty in life, they would not allow themselves to live in the dissipated way they do. Surely truly genteel people would surround themselves with quality living.

However, this does not seem to be the case. Many Messies are very much in tune with the finer aspects of life. Intellect, beauty— Messies do not lack these qualities. What they lack is focus on how their noble ideals relate to their environment.

---

over to her house, I was warned not to touch anything or move around much. This woman was an example of a 10.

As an adult I lived next door to a woman who used to hose down her house after it rained because the rain had splattered dirt on the outside wall. I went into her house. It looked like a model home. I commented that she must have just had her kitchen cabinets painted. "About seven years ago," was her reply.

Don't ask me how she did it. Her husband spent a lot of time down the street in a bar and took his shoes off at the front door when he did come in. That's a 10 for you—hard to live with.

We don't want to be either a ½ or a 10. Those who rate from 4–6 are those successful, average housekeepers we aim to be. Their houses are satisfactory most of the time, varying with the circumstances. They don't even think a lot about their houses; they just keep them up. A 4–6 would not be likely to come to a Messies Anonymous class unless she was dissatisfied with being average and wanted to be a more efficient housekeeper. Some have come and found the class helpful.

The 7–9 group are Cleanies. This is a generally wonderful group, and I admire its members a great deal. Like model homes, their houses act as something of an inspiration to me even though I will never reach their pinnacle of perfection.

Some Cleanies enjoy keeping their homes at the high level they maintain. Some do not. Some tell me that they wish they could relax more when it comes to housekeeping. Recently, a Cleanie from Ireland told me that she and her friends work all day to keep their homes in pristine order. "My house is perfect from top to bottom at this moment," she said and then added with a groan, "I wish I could stop working on the house and have a good time with my family and friends. I can never stop. It's always on my mind."

With her face strained as she thought of her problem, she asked me if I could provide some help for people like her and her friends.

We Messies know we don't want to overdo like that. We know we definitely want to improve our situation. But how do we begin?

Housekeeping Level	Telltale Sign
0	No one cares to enter your house.
1	Fools rush in where angels fear to tread.
2	If you had to, you could find at least one clean towel.
3	The dishes are clean, but stay out of the upstairs bath!
4	At least once a week, everything's spotless—for a day.
5	You can read a book without overwhelming guilt.
6	The minister's wife can drop over unexpectedly without panicking you.
7	You can hold elaborate luncheons twice a week and have everything neat by 3:30 p.m.
8	You gave away the dog and made the kids understand.
9	Your children aren't allowed downstairs, except to eat (neatly).
10	No one dares to enter your house.

10

Goal Setting

He Who Aims at Nothing Is Likely to Hit It

> *You got to have a dream.*
> *If you don't have a dream,*
> *How you gonna have a dream come true?*

OSCAR HAMMERSTEIN, *SOUTH PACIFIC*

If you don't know where you are going, there is no need to start. Perhaps those of us who had Cleanie mothers have one advantage over those who did not. We know how nice a clean house can be. How lovely it is to have one's drawers neat and tidy. How lovely it is to bring friends home and be proud of the decor and the order.

If your mother did not leave you this legacy, then you can pick it up now from friends whose homes you admire. In our church we have frequent get-togethers in homes of various members of the congregation. At first I thought they had just fixed things up for the church get-together, but when I went into the back bathroom or the garage, or chanced to look in an open closet door, and saw the same neatness there that I saw in the more public areas, I was sure this was the way they always lived.

Halloween was also a revelation. At that time, when mothers walked their little tots around trick-or-treating, I would move the clutter from the living room door out of sight and down the hall. Then I would close the curtains that revealed the other parts of the house. From the vantage point of the front door, things were passable.

But I would see that my neighbors didn't have their homes curtained off. Their windows were open for viewing and, perhaps more startling to me, their homes were lovely. I didn't have time for beauty. I was just surviving. I began to dream that my house could be that way. I envied the well-placed figurine, the uncluttered space. It was a good envy. It made me want to change.

Daydreaming can be an excellent thing. Studies have shown that people who are high achievers are frequently daydreamers. They use daydreaming as a method of goal setting. You can do that, too. Use creative daydreaming to work for you. My daydream is something like this:

> I see clean, shining tabletops warmly reflecting the lamp and the well-chosen items on the tables. I see sunlight and leafy shadows playing across the vacuumed rug. I see my favorite colors artfully used, affirming that this is a place for me to be happy and comfortable.
>
> I see my family moving happily in their home, clothes and food easily provided. I see myself full of energy because I am in control.
>
> I see myself developing and growing stronger in spiritual ways, because I have time and energy for the Spirit. I thank the

Lord for the opportunity to live up to my unique potential for my own pleasure and that of those around me.

Get out a piece of paper and write out your own daydream. How do you want your house to look? Once you have written it down, you are on your way to achieving that goal.

Setting Goals

It is valuable to state your goal specifically. When I set out to gain control of my house, I had only a general, foggy idea that things had to be "better." But as I gave it further thought, I hit upon a goal statement that says it all: "I want my house to be like Marcella's."

You have already met Marcella, one of my Cleanie friends. I was at Marcella's today, around ten in the morning. Marcella was caring for her six-year-old, home from kindergarten, her five-month-old baby, and a friend's year-old baby. What an invitation to chaos! But as usual, the house was spotless and even prettier than I remembered it. Obviously it isn't because she keeps people out; she is always willing to share her home with children and adults alike. Seeing that inspires me to keep going.

Although my house may never be exactly like Marcella's, I want it to express the same neat, shining, and pretty atmosphere. As a matter of fact, people have come into my house since I have changed and actually said, "My, your house is so pretty!" That makes it all worth it.

On the same piece of paper on which you wrote your creative daydream, write a sentence or two stating your goal. If you write it, your muscles will already be in the act and you will be starting to change. Set a five-year goal and a life goal too.

Vaslav Nijinsky, one of the great ballet stars of all time, is legendary even today though he lived in a time when there were no moving pictures of his dancing. It is said that he could leap higher than any other dancer, five feet into the air, and hover there a second or two. Now, on the surface, this would seem to be an impossible task. When people asked him how he could do this, he replied, "It's easy! I just made up my mind to do it." He could not do it the day after he decided to, of course, but once a determined individual sets a goal, he finds a way to reach it. And he did.

In athletics, successful goal setters abound. Tom Dempsey, who shares the record for kicking the longest field goal in NFL history, hobbled onto the field because he has only half a foot and wears special shoes. But he did the job. Boy, did he do the job! Obstacles are insignificant to a determined goal setter. They do not disappear; they are just overcome.

I was watching the televised Olympics when a young American runner who had come in second was being interviewed. He said he would continue to train for four more years for the next Olympics, when he hoped to win the gold medal.

The interviewer asked, "When you put yourself under the strain of training for four years for one race, what is likely to give out first? The legs?"

"No," was the reply, "the mind."

"The secret of success," said Benjamin Disraeli, "is constancy of purpose." Winston Churchill said it another way: "Never give in, never give in, never, never, never, never—in nothing, great or small, large or petty—never give in except to convictions of honor and good sense."

The hardest part is keeping one's goal in view when the going gets tough and the end is not in sight. That's why it is so important to write it down. If it is written, you have made a stronger commitment. If you have not written your goal yet, you can write it in the margin of this book. If you have written it on paper, store it in this book so you'll know where to locate it.

Reaching Your Goals

To reach this goal, you will need to welcome the three Cs into your life.

Change

There have to be changes if things are going to improve. But change is hard to bring about. The way things are is at least familiar and somewhat comfortable, however unsatisfactory.

Perhaps the hardest changes to make are in the mind. The ideas that "creative people are messy" or that "a person with three preschool children cannot keep a neat house" or worst of all, "I am hopeless," must be changed or no improvement will come.

The truth is that we are all made in the image of God. God is not a God of disorder. This means first, we are not happy living in disorder because it is against our natures and second, we do have the power to control and order our lives.

When God first put Adam in the world, he told him to have dominion. We need to take that position in our homes: We are going to have dominion. I believe it is God's will that we take control of the portion of our lives that is our responsibility and rule it competently and well.

Commitment

Commitment involves dedication to a project. If your house is really important, dedicate yourself to the task of cleaning it up. Put it at the top of your list of priorities.

Control

I have already told you what nice people Messies are. Some of us are too nice for our own good, and for the good of our families. We are the room mothers, the Cub Scout leaders, and the Sunday school teachers.

We need to use good *judgment*. It is hard to suggest cutting back on such obviously worthwhile activities. Nevertheless, I am going to suggest that you do cut back. The good is enemy of the best.

Our first responsibility is our home, not for the sake of the house but for the sake of ourselves and our families. The home is the base from which we reach out into the world. When our base is in order and we have a schedule of maintenance, then we can begin to add a little at a time until we see how much we can handle.

Here's where control takes over. If you have been known as a community worker, people will continue to ask you to do jobs. You must take control of your life. Make your decision in the light of your priorities and if necessary, say, "No, I'm sorry I won't be able to help you on that."

Sometimes you can suggest an alternative. If you are asked to bake cookies for a class party, tell them you will be willing to buy them. If requested to take part in a money-raising event, make a donation instead.

The hardest person to say no to is yourself. Your hobbies of ceramics, gardening, writing, painting, and friendships vie so pleasantly for control. If your top priority for right now is organizing the house, promise yourself and your friends that later, when things are different, you will return to your old acquaintances and activities refreshed and happy.

You have only a limited amount of time and energy. Spend it where it will help accomplish your goals.

The Diamond of Success

In housekeeping as in any other job we set out to do, there are factors that set the successful achiever apart from the frustrated wheel spinner.

What sets Cleanies apart from Messies? They have a formula for success whether they are aware of it or not.

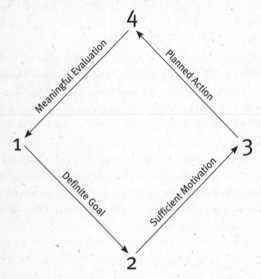

1. Definite Goal

A goal must be specific in order to be meaningful or useful. Just to say, "I don't want to live this way anymore" is not enough.

How do you want to live? Make it clear by deciding something like this: "I see myself being able to have friends over anytime without three days' work." "I see myself waking up in the morning with the house under control and I see myself with a plan to keep it under control."

Emerson said, "Thoughts rule the world." Make your thoughts concrete. Even if you have done it before, write on this line your statement of your goal for yourself.

My goal for my house is _____

_____

Remember: "He who aims at nothing will likely hit it."

2. Sufficient Motivation

Athletes know that 90 percent of preparation is mental and 10 percent is physical. They know that many times they lose because they beat themselves; they psych themselves out. The main thing is to have a winning attitude. In order to win in athletics you must expect to win.

Use what is called the movie technique to get yourself going in the morning. See yourself doing the jobs you have planned, leaving the house in order, and returning to a supportive house.

Now mix what you see with emotion while you are seeing it. Feel determined as you see yourself working; feel happy when you see your job completed.

3. Planned Action

Halfhearted doing will doom us to failure.

There is a verse in the Bible that says, "And whatever you do, do it heartily, as to the Lord," but the big part of our problem is lack of knowing what to do and when to do it. That's why the Mount Vernon Method and the Flipper Method, described in part 3, are so important. They give us a plan for getting the house organized and keeping it that way. We can wear ourselves out just deciding what to do if we don't have a predetermined plan.

Ways to Keep Your Dream Alive

People have different learning styles. Tap into the method that is the best for you.

1. If you are visually inspired: Get a picture out of a magazine. Use it as your inspiration.
2. If you are an auditory person: Listen daily to the Messies Anonymous inspiration tape, "Create Your Dream and Live It," or make your own encouraging audiotape to listen to repeatedly.
3. If you are kinesthetically and tactilely oriented: Go to model homes or the houses of friends who have their act together. Walk through, touching and experiencing the spaces, colors, light, etc.
4. If you are very verbal: In a journal, write about your dreams and goals daily.

Most of us use all of these modalities to some extent. Get a picture, listen to tapes, visit model homes, write in a journal. Tap into them all. Motivation is a terrible thing to waste. You need to do everything you can to keep going till you reach your dream.

And once you decide what to do, do it heartily.

Remember the older woman who was asked for the secret of her lifelong success? She replied: "When I works, I works hard; and when I sits, I sits loose." Work hard; *then* sit loose.

One word of warning: Don't plan to do so much in the beginning that you wear yourself out and quit. Pace yourself and take a day off each week.

4. Meaningful Evaluation

One temptation is to put a plan into motion and just keep on keeping on with it simply because it is our plan and not because it works. We need to stop and evaluate whether it works.

Ed Koch, the former mayor of New York City, was known for asking frequently, "How am I doing?" Stop and ask yourself, "How am I doing?"

Now that you have your goal set firmly in your mind and have written it down as well, let's take a look at the five problem areas that often afflict the Messie housekeeper. Afterward, you will be given an exercise to help you determine which of these areas is causing you the most difficulty.

11

Five Pitfalls for the Wanderer in Messieland

If you want a golden rule that will fit everybody, this is it: Have nothing in your houses that you do not know to be useful or believe to be beautiful.

WALTER KITTEREDGE

Problems with housekeeping seem to fall into five main categories. Some of them overlap a bit, but I am sure you can recognize them easily and pick out the ones that relate to you most strongly.

Pitfalls

1. Storage or Organization

This includes maintaining orderly drawers and closets and the storage of seldom-used items such as Christmas things and lightbulbs. Storage is the basis for what is to follow in other areas of cleaning. If you don't have a place for everything, how can you put it away?

Few people see whether or not we have messy closets, but they do see the results of it. If you have to look and look for the phone book or keys or whatever, this needs work.

2. Neatness

Some people tell me they are disorganized in their closets and drawers but have neat-looking rooms. This is difficult for me to understand since the same things that made me messy inside the closets made me messy outside them too.

A neatness problem is best identified by our feelings when people drop in unexpectedly. Much visiting has been done on the front porch because we weren't ready for unexpected callers. Many invitations have not been issued because it would take too much work to clean and organize. This is unfortunate because Messies are frequently warm, sociable people who would enjoy sharing their homes with others and entertaining friends. But the house won't allow it!

3. Paper

Where do all the papers come from? Children bring them home from school. Newsboys deliver them. The mailman brings his stack. Magazines come. We pick them up in stores. And occasionally people stick them under our windshields when we are at the store.

But we don't mind, do we? Papers have such fascinating stuff on them. Some of them have ideas, and Messies are very practical. Papers can also be important. They can have to do with taxes, children's school activities, and so forth. We are especially infatuated with papers. And we love to keep them.

4. Bills and Banking

This is an area of life that requires organization or it falls apart. A bill makes no demands for a while, so it is easy to set aside and forget until it has gone into oblivion. Banking is the same way. The statement comes so quietly and so neatly packaged that the tendency is to let it stay closed up in its little envelope. So long as it is there somewhere we are comfortable until the bill is overdue or bank account overdrawn.

But that doesn't quite solve the checking problem. Some people attending my seminars have told me they keep two accounts and switch back and forth as the need arises to keep current with the balance in an account. One woman told me she has even changed banks, letting one account stand long enough to get it under control and to let all the checks come in. That was the only way she could know how much money she had in the account.

I understand this. For me the detail and tedium of the checking process is difficult. Since I am distractible, I do not find it an automatic process to record every deduction and every withdrawal. Failure to do so, though, can cause havoc in a checking account.

Online banking and bill paying have revolutionized the problem for those who use them consistently. Calling the bank or checking in via computer can clarify a lot of confusion.

But no machines automatically solve the problem. Only good systems responsibly followed by responsible human beings will keep bills and banking under control.

5. Collecting

What I have in mind is the keen desire to gather lots of things because they "might come in handy someday." Or to keep them for the sake of the past.

The word *collecting* is perhaps not the best word to describe this problem. *Collecting* indicates some order or design, which in this case is lacking.

Why do we love to collect so many things and have such a hard time throwing them out? Either we do it for the past or for the future. Certainly it isn't for the present, since the present is suffering because of all this stuff we are trying to live with.

We feel we have to hold on to things from the past because we are trying to preserve a beautiful memory. The things we keep are attached in our minds to some important person or event in our lives, and we keep them out of respect. This is a particular problem when the person whose things we are keeping has died. One of my seminar students felt compelled to keep several houses full of furniture because they were from the estates of deceased loved ones. The same woman had four closets full of clothes four sizes too big from her admired, deceased mother-in-law, whose memory she wished to preserve. A widow I knew felt that if she threw away anything that had belonged to her husband she would be throwing away part of him. My guess is that anyone who loved us would be the first to urge us to live our lives in the present and not try to hang on to the past.

We also try to keep things for the future—just in case we ever need them. We save for possible needs or emergencies that might come. Don't sacrifice the present for the future. That's no healthier than living in the past.

We also keep things because they are valuable. Everything has some value, no matter how small. I had occasion to take metal bones out of several bras. Do you know that I was reluctant to throw them away? *There must be something they would be good for*, I thought. *Maybe I ought to save them. Perhaps I could glue them together to make Christmas ornaments.*

It's true, there might be some use for them, but no one has appointed me keeper of everything that might have some value. That is too big a burden to bear. I threw them away happily when I realized I didn't have to think that way anymore.

My mother who, as you already know, is a Cleanie, told me of her latest garage sale. "It's so nice in the house now. I got rid of all the things I didn't use. Now the closet floors are empty and only what I need is in the drawers. It's wonderful, wonderful, wonderful!" From staying with her on visits I can tell you that living that way is wonderful. There is freedom in having no more than you need, no more than you can control.

But the collecting impulse is hard to control because on the surface it seems so logical. Why *not* keep that yarn? Someday you may learn to knit, and it will be wonderful to have your own supply already! (*If* you can find it.) Why not keep all prescription medicines? Someday your child may be ill in the middle of the night and the doctor may say that only one medicine will help him. You'll look in the cabinet and find that you have that very medicine, even if it is ten years old. The doctor will say that it is better to have ten-year-old medicine than none at all, and you will give it to your child and he will be saved. So, you see, it is dangerous to throw anything away.

The problem with this thinking is that it just doesn't work. We gather and gather and gather good things, and some things that are not so good. Soon the pile gets out of control, and we can't find what we want when we need it.

Things control us and our lives. We begin to make adjustments in our way of life to accommodate all the "stuff" we

---

Junk Animals

As you walk through your house, look around. You have old, caged-up junk animals wanting relief from their long imprisonments. They don't want to be there. Treat them with dignity, treat yourself with dignity, and let them go.

- Old lipstick and nail polish
- Broken kitchen utensils
- Good but unused kitchen utensils
- Old paint
- Outgrown clothes
- Threadbare towels and bed linens

---

have. We tell ourselves that we *can't* throw anything out. We end up with so much that it is a monumental task to clean or organize.

I am not saying that everything must go. But the collecting mania has to be controlled if we are ever going to get off this unmerry merry-go-round.

Not everyone wants to break the collecting cycle, but there's a good chance you do. You bought this book because you want to change and because you know there is more to life than amassing great globs of junk. You can avoid all of the pitfalls and problems that are part of the habit of hoarding.

A Personal Evaluation

One way to start is to identify which of the five pitfalls is your greatest problem. The following evaluation exercise will help you get a handle on your strengths as well as your weaknesses. Respond to each statement with the answer that best reflects your situation today. Resist the temptation to give what you think is the "proper" reply. Then, using the answer key, interpret your evaluation to see which of these problems needs the most attention in overcoming your "Messie" status.

Answer each of the following true or false.

1. It is hard for me to throw away newspapers because I might have missed something good in them.
2. I am successful in using coupons.
3. I have to work all day to have dinner guests that night.
4. I follow a plan for bill paying and have a place to keep the receipts.
5. I still have my high school dance program (or the equivalent) somewhere in the house.
6. I have medicine over five years old in my medicine cabinet.
7. I know how much I have in my checking account.
8. I keep my bedroom door closed when I have guests.
9. Having houseguests is next to impossible.
10. I know what I would do with an extra shoelace or lightbulb.
11. I keep magazine issues that have good articles in them.
12. I clip newspaper articles but don't have any special plan for keeping and finding them.
13. My photo snapshots are under control.
14. My matching sheets and pillowcases are together.
15. I hate unexpected visitors to drop in.
16. I decide what to have for meals as I shop.
17. My cleaning materials are close to where I use them.
18. Cleaning the stove is part of my regular cleaning.
19. There are pieces of jewelry I can't find.
20. I buy things I don't need just in case I might need them someday.

If you had no problem, your answers would match the ones below, which are sorted into five categories. Mark each one you missed.

Answers

Collecting	Paper	Organization	Banking	Neatness
1. F	2. T	10. T	4. T	3. F
5. F	12. F	14. T	7. T	8. F
6. F	13. T	16. F		9. F
11. F		17. T		15. F
20. F		18. T		
		19. F		
Missed x 4	Missed x 6	Missed x 3	Missed x 10	Missed x 5
Score: ___	Score: ___	Score: ___	Score: ___	Score: ___

Evaluations

The problem area in which you made the highest score is likely to be the one you most need to work on. Still, this is not always the case. You may feel some other area causes you more difficulty. In that case, go with your intuition.

Now list your problem areas from the biggest to the smallest. As you go about implementing your new housekeeping system, you will be aware of which areas require the most concentration on your part.

Biggest Problem 1 _____
                 2 _____
                 3 _____
                 4 _____
Smallest Problem 5 _____

Once you have isolated your specific problem areas, it will be easier for you to take command of them. Now you are ready to get started on the road to good housekeeping. In the next section of this book I am going to share with you exactly how I took command of my house, the system that helped me get organized, and the tools that help me stay in control.

PART 3

The System

12

The Mount Vernon Method

How I Took Command

*A man can succeed at almost anything for
which he has unlimited enthusiasm.*

CHARLES SCHWAB

The first thing you need to know to organize your home is the
Mount Vernon Method. Some years ago during my desperate search for help, a Cleanie friend told me about the Mount
Vernon Method. While touring George Washington's estate,
my friend had been so impressed with the maintenance that
she made a point of asking the woman who was in charge of
housekeeping about the method they used.

The housekeeper explained that she directs her cleaners to
start at the front door and work their way around the periphery
of the room. When one room is finished, they proceed to the
next, doing everything that needs to be done in each room so

the rooms are left clean and organized. They dust and wax from the time they come to work early in the day until it is time for the public to arrive. A few minutes before opening time the workers collect their boxes of cleaning supplies and leave. Each day they begin where they left off the day before and keep going from room to room until it is quitting time.

Making Those Hard Decisions

It is easy to clean Mount Vernon. George is not there to mess it up! I decided not to use the method for dusting and polishing, for cleaning walls, drapes, upholstery, or carpets. First I needed to get organized. So I used it for that. I started at the front door.

The first item of furniture beside my front door was a lamp table with one small drawer. After I had cleaned that little drawer, throwing away several very old school calendars, old classified ads, and a lot of junk, I felt I could do anything.

This was the first time I had begun to make decisions. Until then things could come and go of their own accord. I was only an observer. No wonder my house was disorganized! Now I was taking charge. This was heady business.

Next was a piece of living room furniture that had six drawers, two of which literally had not been opened for years. I was actually afraid to open them. Why? I think I believed I would not be able to handle what I found—that my decision-making apparatus would be sprung and broken.

But after a good night's rest, I did open the drawers. The challenge turned out to be a paper tiger. I could easily handle the things I found there. There were no terrible decisions to make. I am still surprised at the unreasonable fear I felt about those

114

drawers. I think I had been afraid there would be baby clothes to deal with. My motherly heart grew faint at the thought.

As I continued around the house, I threw out twelve-year-old medicine from my medicine cabinet. In my clothes closet I came across my wedding shoes. They were twenty-three years old, were missing a decorative buckle, and had never fit. However, I thought perhaps someday I might locate the buckle and they might come back in style. (You never can tell, you know. Miracles do happen!) I threw them out. I wasn't going to let the past with its lovely memories muddle today. Messies are hopelessly sentimental.

You have to think about your total house organization, not just memories. We think because we are capable in other ways we can handle a house full of clutter. Yet even the most capable person can't work when things are disorganized. So think organization.

Pacing Yourself

The most important thing about the Mount Vernon Method is that you pace yourself and not overdo. The temptation is to work like a crazy person because of the frustration you feel. Don't start out too fast. You will not be able to accomplish the method in a single day. (It took me three and a half months to "Mount Vernonize" my home.)

Think of this as a marathon as opposed to a sprint. Since a sprint is a short-term race, you start out giving it all you've got. For a marathon, however, you have to conserve at the beginning of the race because you know you have the end to think about. Housekeeping is a marathon, not a sprint. Go slow and steady. Don't start a whole closet if it is too much. Plan to do two shelves at a time if you can handle this better.

Try to work for at least an hour each stint. It helps to have someone else in the room with you as you do this job. It seems to cut down on tension and make decision making easier. When you have done enough for one day, stop. Take one day off each week so you can look forward to a break. I also advise that you leave the kitchen until last. Kitchens aren't for rookies!

Overcoming Obstacles

During my stint with the Mount Vernon Method, I sometimes came to a place I felt I just couldn't tackle. To get around this obstacle, I did two things: (1) I took an extra day off, and (2) I decided to reward myself with something extra special when I finished the "big bad job."

Sometimes, when I came to really sentimental things, I had to stop and honor them. My nicest maternity dress was laid in state for three days on my bed before I folded it gently and put it in a bag to take to the nearest charity for some other happy mother-to-be to enjoy.

It might be useful to think of belongings in this way. Things have a natural lifecycle, just like people do. They start, live, and come to the end of their lives. When they come to the end of their lives with us, we can ritualize their passing. It helps us to grieve and let go. Once I had a group of personal items I knew had to go. I put them in a group and placed a three-by-five-inch index card on them expressing my appreciation for their contributions to my life. After a few days, I moved them out of the house to start their lives anew with someone else.

These techniques kept me going!

Working the Plan

Make a list of three or four items that you plan to do each day before you start Mount Vernonizing (like load the dishwasher and do a load of laundry—always include make the bed). Remember that the method is for organizing, not for heavy cleaning.

Begin at the front door and start with the first piece of furniture you come to that has a nook, cranny, drawer, etc. As you move from one spot to another around the room, take with you three boxes: a giveaway box, a throwaway box, and a put-elsewhere box. Open the first drawer.

Throw away every piece of junk that has accumulated there. Be serious about it. Don't keep the pen that only works half the time; toss the pretty calendar that's already a year old. Your freedom from clutter is more important than they are.

When you find things that are too good to throw out, put them in the giveaway box. And give them away soon! You'll be glad you shared. Two cautions are in order:

1. Don't take anything out of the giveaway box once you've put it in.
2. Don't wait for the perfect time or the perfect person to give it to. Get rid of it right away. Don't save a matchbook for Mary's son who saves matchbooks. Don't even save it for a garage sale unless you have a specific date set for a sale. After that date, give it to your favorite charity.

Be willing to take a risk that you may later want what you discarded. One Messie who is succeeding at becoming a good housekeeper wrote to tell me that the risk is worth it:

I can honestly say that we have never missed anything that we got rid of. We did replace one ancient single bed which we sold and later needed. Cost was seventy-five dollars—a small price for the use of a room for three years. (The bedroom had been so stuffed with junk, it was unused until then!)

Remember that although it may cause temporary pain to throw something out, it causes definite long-term pain to keep it. Tossing it out is mild pain compared with the pain that comes from having to live helplessly with all that clutter. There is an exhilarating feeling of freedom that comes once the decision is made to take control of the house.

The put-elsewhere box is there to keep the things that don't need to be discarded but are in the wrong place. Do not hop up and put them in another place while you are working, because this will break your concentration. You may never return to your job there. Just put them into the box and drag the box around with you as you go from one piece of furniture to another. Put the items in this box away when you finally reach the place where they will be grouped with other similar items.

It does not matter how quickly you complete the Mount Vernon phase. What matters is that you are consistent in your efforts and determination to complete the task. This does not mean that all I had to do to put my house in order was to apply some willpower. Not so! Over the years the willpower method had not worked any better than anything else for me. No, it required a system—and some very special tools.

You may wish to include a fourth box while you are doing the Mount Vernon Method. It is the ambivalence box, a box for things you can't make up your mind about. If you run into a decision that holds you up because you know you should get rid of something but you can hardly bear to do it, put it in this box. When the box is more or less full, put the top on it and take it out to the garage or some other storage place where you will see it often. Write a date on the box in large dark letters. This is the date that you will discard the box. It may be any length of time away that you desire.

During that time, you may go and retrieve any item you decide you want to keep. But if you have not retrieved anything by the date on the box, give the box away unopened. Do not look at or touch the contents. Recent research in the area of hoarding indicates that if the items in the box are seen, you will reconnect to them in an emotional way. The newsletter of the National Study Group on Chronic Disorganization states that when Messies touch their belongings, they seem to "rebond" with them and find it hard to let go.

The ambivalence box gives us time to disconnect with our belongings without feeling as though they have been ripped from our lives.

Note: If you have a house full of so much stuff that this method will not work for you, consult the Mount Vesuvius Method in chapter 15. Then come back to chapter 13 to find out what to do with all those boxes.

13

Simplify, Sort, and Store

The Heart of Organizing

If there is a better solution . . . find it.

THOMAS EDISON

Organizing is basically a simple deal. It is easy to explain; it is easy to understand. But it is not easy to do unless you focus very carefully on three steps that are the heart of organizing. If you understand and apply these three steps consistently, you will be organized.

I'll tell you not only what to do for each step but also how to do it. The how-to is very important because here we build in some of those all-important boundaries that will bolster our organizing abilities.

Strongly resist the temptation to substitute memory for organizing. You know what I mean. "I know where everything is in all of these piles" may be more or less true for some people, but it is a rotten system even when it works. It causes stress, wastes time, works poorly, and has limitations because it can't work when the number of items to remember gets too great. Instead, do deep-down organizational change using these three wonderful steps.

Simplify
Sort
Store

Simplify

Simplify means to separate the things you want to keep from the things that you need to get rid of. We do this by using the Mount Vernon Method.

Sort

You have heard the saying, "A place for everything and everything in its place." This is okay as far as it goes but it leaves out another very important old saying: "Birds of a feather flock together."

1. Group

Here's what this second saying means in relation to setting up a system that works when organizing. Put everything that is alike together in one place as you arrive at that place with your put-elsewhere box. I've already mentioned that many of us who are disorganized have trouble sorting things into workable groups. Here's the answer to that problem. It seems simple, but it is important and powerful because it works.

Have different centers for your items. You can have the photo center, the sewing center, the craft center, the music center, the art center, the baking center, the mailing center, the repair center, etc. Group together all things that relate to that center. Even CDs, DVDs, videotapes, and cassettes can be organized this way.

I used to have a place for everything, but the items were not grouped according to categories. If I wanted to wrap a present, for instance, I had to work hard to assemble the necessary equipment. The hard part was not just getting it rounded up but trying to remember where all the stuff was kept. Often, because there was not any real reason for where the things were kept, they weren't replaced in their designated place after their use. If things went right in this haphazard system, the scissors were in the living room drawer, the tape was in a desk drawer, the wrapping paper was under the bed, the ribbon was in the hall closet. Even if the system worked at its most efficient, it was difficult to get everything assembled. I gave up this ineffective system. Now I have a wrapping center. It is a low flat box designed to hold everything for wrapping, and it fits under the bed.

Scissors and tape are used for many purposes, so it may be necessary to buy several of each so you can have them in each center where they are used. (Now that's a unique idea!)

Sometimes, because of the layout of the house, everything in the same category cannot be stored together. The birds-of-a-feather rule should not be broken lightly, but if you must, split the things into only two groups and *put a note* on each grouping stating where the other part of the group is.

2. Label

Actually make placards with typing paper and broad-tipped markers. Write the names of the centers in large letters. Tape the sign on the wall behind the pile, on the box the group is in, or on the pile itself. As you are dragging your put-elsewhere box around with you, you can drop off your items when you get to where they belong in your house. The placard idea is very important. Don't try to keep the various centers and their locations in your memory as you work around your house. Relying on memory is ineffective and stressful. Those large placards with the big writing will help keep you straight.

Let's face it. You don't see well-organized people with labels all over their houses, do you? No, because they don't need them. Messies do. No, not in the living room! Not where company coming to visit can see, but in strategic places that serve us well. Usually these are hidden away behind closed doors or in private areas of the house.

Labeling helps in several ways:

- It makes our organizational system "official" and for that reason we are more likely to use it. Labeling also helps us to remember what the system was that we devised.

- It tells other members of our family where to put things. It also indicates to them that we are really serious about organizing.

- It helps us to see patterns of organizing that we would likely overlook otherwise. In this way it hones our organizational skills.

Store

Unless this part is done right, the other two parts just will not work. There are five cardinal rules for storing things successfully.

1. Have Enough Storage Places

Sometimes people will have books all over the floor, tables, and bed and not realize that the source of their problem is a simple lack of bookcases (and an overabundance of books that need to be given away). Piles of paper sneak up on people and they fail to realize that they need to get a filing cabinet or a larger filing cabinet (as well as get rid of a bunch of papers). Don't say that you can't afford to buy storage equipment. For some reason, disorganized people resist buying to meet their storage needs and yet spend freely on less crucial items. Maybe that is your situation. I know it was mine until I realigned my priorities and put clutter control at the top of my budget.

2. Keep Stored Items Visible

Buy clear plastic shoe boxes, clear Lucite magazine holders (if you must keep magazines), and, for some occasions, see-through file folders. Keep things out on shelves where they are easily visible.

To avoid using files in which papers seem to disappear, some people use a system of stacking trays (labeled, of course) to keep their papers easily in view. This may work well to a limited degree but not at all if you have a large number of papers to keep up with or if you have limited space. In this case you will need a filing cabinet.

3. "Containerize" Your Belongings

Containers are more boundaries. Don't just lay your belongings on a shelf; they will get away. I don't know how they do it. If they are not in some kind of container, preferably a clear one that you have labeled, they manage to disorganize themselves during the night and all your sincere efforts are for naught.

4. Label What You Store

Here are those labels again. Next to my family, I love labels most because they are so helpful. Make easy-to-read labels with dark markers on something like a three-by-five-inch card showing what is in your boxes, on your shelves, or in your files. Attach those labels on the front of the box, on the shelf, or on the front of your file drawer. Not only will you know what is in that spot, but those you live with will too. The fact that you have a label on the storage spot will encourage you to put things back there where they belong instead of dropping them in convenient spots where they don't go.

5. Store in Proximity to Use

In the kitchen, the dishes go by the dishwasher, the food items by the stove. The more often they are used, the closer they are stored to where you work. The can opener and cooking utensils (often used) are easily in reach, and the turkey roaster (seldom used) is stored up high in the cabinet. In the home office, the most used files are at arm's reach from the chair and the archival materials are at a distance from the desk.

Storing the Leftovers

You know and I know that no matter how much we get rid of during the dejunking of our house using the Mount Vernon Method and no matter how well we store things in our kitchens and closets, we will always have things left over that we want to keep in storage. Maybe we keep them, planning to thin them out later. The rule is: Everything needs to be properly stored for easy retrieval, whether you plan to get rid of it later or not.

Get White Boxes

Getting the right storage boxes is the first step. Don't get used boxes at the grocery store or wherever. They are ugly and they vary in size. And they don't have good tops. We are going to keep these boxes in our home. We want to take pride in how our storage area looks.

Buy white boxes from an office supply store. They are the kind with some writing on the sides for recordkeeping, used by bankers to store papers and file folders. The tops are easily removed. Often they are called banker's boxes.

Sort the Stuff

Let me congratulate you on getting to this point. If you have not already grouped the things you want to store, do it now. Dresser drawers, closets, and cabinets hold the things used often. Use boxes for storage of excess. Place as many opened boxes around you as you think you will have groups. Tape a large sign on each box telling what that box will hold. Then, as quickly as you can, fill the boxes and put the lids on.

Label the Boxes

Now, remove the large sign and instead affix a three-by-five-inch index card indicating the category of the box (e.g., Winter Clothes, Toys, Old Newspapers, Holiday Decorations). List the items in the box. Things like blue wool sweater, gray sweat suit, black skirt, etc. could follow on the card headed by Winter Clothes.

Do this to all the boxes.

Group the Boxes

Now stack boxes that are alike together. All of the clothes boxes, papers boxes, and toys boxes are grouped together. Label them to indicate what the group is. For example, the three clothes boxes can be C–1, C–2, C–3. Store these boxes, which are now grouped together and labeled, out of the way. The fact that they are white and neat will make them look unobtrusive, like a white wall extension.

Make a Master List

These boxes will be stored in some out-of-the-way place. It may be inconvenient to go to the boxes to read the cards on the outside of the boxes to see if your gray slacks or some other item is stored in one of the boxes. To solve that problem, make duplicate index cards and store them where they are easily accessed, like in an index card box. Now you can locate any item you want just by flipping through the cards. They will tell you that those slacks are in C–3.

If you have a computer, keep your list on a word processing document and use the FIND or SEARCH command to locate what you are looking for quickly.

Strange and Wonderful Things Begin to Happen

You will notice a strange thing happening as you sort like things together. As your craft items begin to gather at the Craft placard, you may be amazed at how much stuff you have. You could start a nursery school. You didn't know that you had eight bottles of glue, three hot glue guns, a large bag of yarn—and on it goes. When you see how much duplication you have, it is easier to simplify.

You will also notice that a strange thing happens as you store and label your goods. Once you can be sure that you can easily locate what you need when you need it, you will begin to feel that it is not necessary to keep duplicates in the house so that you can find one if the other is lost. You will trust your system. The other will not be lost. The result is that the storage step helps you to get rid of stuff, to do the hardest of all steps, the simplify step.

Somewhere in talking about all of these organizational systems, you have got to be asking yourself whether setting up all of these systems is more work than it is worth. Is it worth it? The answer is "Yes! Yes! A thousand times, yes!" For me, it is more than worth it. Nothing could be so stressful as living the way I was when:

I couldn't find my clothes to get dressed without a search party

Keys were often lost

Papers were so permanently misplaced that it was the same as not having them

I endured more insults from my chaotic house than most people can imagine

Matching socks, receipts to return things (even the things to be returned), school papers to be signed and returned, clean underwear when needed on a consistent basis—all of these were unknown in my house. You'd better believe that using the systems I have developed for my own sanity is worth it! They give me power over what would otherwise be a discouraging and topsy-turvy life.

You may not need them all. You may need to develop others that meet your own specific situation. Don't develop more than you really need. Don't be more organized than you have to be, but don't be any less.

For more help on organizing things and your time, consult "Resources" at the end of this book or contact Messies Anonymous about the informative book *The Whiz Bang Guide on How to Organize Time and Things: Specific Strategies for Forgetful and Disorganized Folks,* which explains these and other important organizing systems in detail.

When all of those birds of a feather begin to flock together, the reforming Messie is likely to get a shock. There may be a lot more birds alike than anticipated.

When she gathered her crafts together, Mimi's arts and craft center overflowed with craft paper, glue sticks, trim and beads, and enough of this and that to stock a preschool.

Brad corralled his tools. You guessed it, he had more screwdrivers, hammers, vice-grips, and pliers than he could use in three lifetimes. Because he had never kept them in one place consistently, he often bought new tools when he couldn't locate missing ones.

Sorting things often makes it much easier to simplify.

14

The Flipper Keeps It in Order

*As one goes through life, one learns that if you
don't paddle your own canoe, you don't move.*

KATHARINE HEPBURN

Any Messie can tell you that the real problem of housekeeping
is not getting the house in order; it's keeping it that way! The
Mount Vernon Method will help you get it in order. The Flipper
will help you keep it that way.

The Key to Maintenance

I call the Flipper the Magic Key to Maintenance. There really is
something magic about the Flipper: it works, and for this kind
of organizational activity, lists don't!

The Flipper is the heart of the Messies Anonymous organizational program. Many books on housekeeping say, "Make a

schedule of daily activities for the house." Sometimes they then give a sample list so that you can get the idea.

Well, I used to make lists, usually at the insistence of my frazzled husband, who kept repeating in a comatose way, "Something has to be done."

Then I either put the list in a pile where it would be "safe" and lost it, or I attached it to the refrigerator where I got so used to seeing it I no longer "saw" it and didn't miss it when it slid down between the refrigerator and the counters.

One reason I didn't use these lists is because I didn't really trust that they were good lists. I didn't respect them. Maybe they were poor lists. Maybe I didn't have every job listed and at the right intervals.

Then too, the lists looked sloppy. They were handwritten and irregular, like everything I tend to do is. Who could respect a flimsy, messy, handwritten piece of paper that purported to tell me how to live? I resented that stupid list forced on me by grim necessity!

But a system is necessary. Some people use other systems, such as cards in a box or computer programs. If a list or any other system works for you, great. Stick with what works. But nothing I had tried was working for me.

One day when I was in the bathtub deep in thought, the idea of the Flipper dawned. My desire is that you will be able to set up your own Flipper with ease by reading this explanation.

Starting Out

The Flipper System puts you on an easy-to-keep daily maintenance schedule. The house will not always be perfect, but with the Flipper it will always be maintained at an acceptable level. After I started using the Mount Vernon Method in conjunction with a few daily jobs from my own Flipper System, my house showed a remarkable change in only three weeks' time. It is important to realize, however, that you cannot use the Flipper successfully until you have Mount Vernonized your home.

The key is to keep it simple. Being perfectionists, being smart, highly motivated people, we overdo. We set up such a complicated system that it sinks under the weight of our overplanning. I am going to give you the streamlined system. You can expand on it if you wish to keep a more highly organized house.

Get the Flipper and Cards

First, get the two main things you need:

1. A photo album that has plastic sleeves arranged in a staggered series and attached to a larger, heavier sheet of card stock. Since it is in book form, it sits on the shelf for easy access.

    The availability of these albums fluctuates. Sometimes you can find them easily at camera shops, drugstores, or variety stores. At other times they are almost impossible to find.

    The SuperFlipper Kit is always available from Messies Anonymous. Look in "Resources" for more information about obtaining it from us.

2. Cards that go into the plastic sleeves. Often the cards are included in the album. If not, index cards work.

Put the Cards in the Flipper

Each card stands for a day and fits in order in the album. You should have enough cards for four weeks—plus a few more for other things.

First decide what you want to do daily. Write that on four cards. Each daily card stands at the beginning of each week. Now put cards Sunday through Saturday in their sleeves following the daily card. You will have four of these sequences of daily and day-of-the-week cards.

Distribute Jobs onto the Cards

So far, it has been easy. Now comes the decision making. But it doesn't have to be too hard if you don't overdo.

Daily Cards

Pull the cards out of the plastic sleeves one at a time so that you can write on them. Fill in three or so daily activities for yourself and at least one for every member of your household on your daily list. Consider what needs doing in relation to the dishes, kitchen, mail, meals, maybe bathroom and laundry, on a daily basis.

If you are the woman of the house, do not do all of the work just because it is easier to do it yourself or because of old habits. Husbands, teens, other adults in the household, and little children can all do something. Don't shortchange their abilities to contribute substantially. It is not fair to you or to them.

My book *Neat Mom, Messie Kids* offers a teamwork system to get every family member into the housework game.

Day-of-the-Week Cards

List one cleaning (do a load of wash, vacuum the living room rug) or organizing activity (pay bills, straighten room) per person on each day-of-the-week card.

Set up a chart to distribute the jobs over a four-week period. Some jobs may only need to be done once a month, like paying bills. Others may need to be done twice a week, like bathrooms.

Don't get keyed up about choosing jobs. Whatever you do will be more than is getting done now. Just disperse a variety of activities in a more or less random way. This is not brain surgery.

If each member in a family of four does one day-of-the-week job over four weeks, that adds up to 112 jobs done! That's impressive. A little done consistently adds up to a lot. If you live alone, less needs to be done. You will be doing twenty-eight jobs in four weeks consistently. Once you have an idea what needs doing when, and a general idea of who you would like to do it, meet with the family for finalization.

This system has two strong features: (1) doing one day-of-the-week job each day is not overwhelming, and (2) sharing the work equally seems fair. Who can argue successfully with a system with those characteristics?

I could go into a lot of detail about how to do each little bit, but then I would be going against my admonition to you to keep this simple. Just do it. You can adjust as you go along if you leave out something or put in too much.

Flipper to the Rescue

One reason the Flipper works as well as it does is because it helps us solve several challenges that we Messies grapple with.

1. *Memory.* The Flipper remembers for us what is to be done each day. Just look at the card. The less we have to carry things around in our head, the freer we are to live in the present without distraction.

2. *Decision making.* Once the decisions are made and the jobs recorded on the cards, we are free from having to decide daily.

3. *Boundaries.* Once we mark off the jobs from the card for that day, we are done. And we know that we are done. Without those cards to tell us we are through for the day, we could keep on forever, or feel that we should. The Flipper supplies those wonderful boundaries that we tend to ignore.

If you skip a day (or days) don't go back to catch up. Just move on from the day you are on.

Write this on the top card in the Flipper so that it is always in view.

Man may work from sun to sun,
But when I finish my card,
My work is done.

Follow Up on the Work

Here is the hard part, especially in the beginning. The buck stops with you. You need to make sure each person does his or her job each day. To do that, you need to obtain two things:

1. A paper clip to mark the day you are working on so each person can be sure which day to look at. Just slip it on the card.

2. A water-soluble nonpermanent marking pen to mark on the plastic sleeve. Because the pen is water soluble, you can wipe the plastic clean with a damp cloth to start the next month.

The person who is doing the job marks off his or her job when it is done. The jobs should be done before dinner so you can inspect them before you eat. This is a nice way of saying that you can't eat if you haven't done your job.

From time to time, some family members may mark off a job as done that hasn't really been done. (This is unbelievable, I know.) Remember, people don't do what you expect; they do what you inspect. This reality is a part of life.

Motivating Yourself

If this system is going to break down, it will be because you as the supervisor have lost the will to follow through. Old habits are hard to break. Your family may grumble. They may mutiny. You may get tired of doing your jobs and supervising theirs.

It is up to you. If you want a new way of life, the Flipper can provide the way about as easily as anything.

There is no system that takes the place of personal involvement and effort. Nothing comes without effort. At this point, it may be a good idea to remember the saying, "If it's to be, it's up to me."

Menu Cards on the Flipper

You probably have more blank sleeves to work with after you have filled in the basic organizational part of the Flipper. This gives the nice opportunity to use those cards for the menu-planning system. Many women love this part of the Flipper and find it saves a lot of time and confusion.

I originally came up with the idea from something I read about Ethel Kennedy. She makes up two weeks of menus, goes through them, then starts again at the beginning for the next two weeks. That's what we do. But we outdo Ethel and plan four weeks of menus!

You might say, "Won't that get monotonous?" Not really. Studies show that without planning, 80 percent of the time the same ten dishes are used over and over again. It is not easy to think of twenty-eight different dishes—seven dinners a week for four weeks. You may wish to repeat a dish—spaghetti, hamburgers, or whatever your family favorites are—more than once during the four-week period. One day a week can be left open to take advantage of whims, gourmet recipes, or seasonal specials.

You can also change your menus every few months if you wish. Each week's menu is put on a separate card and stored in the Flipper. Now you have a permanent menu. From this permanent menu you can make a permanent shopping list, one for each week's menu. I don't know about you, but I hate to make shopping lists! Now we don't have to. Simply store the shopping list in the plastic sleeve on the back of the menu card and slip it out to take to the grocery store when you go shopping. Or, if you wish, you can put a duplicate page in your notebook so you can have it if you decide to stop at the store unexpectedly (the notebook is described later).

One other convenience is possible with the menu plan. Let us assume you have some dishes that require a recipe. Instead of looking up the recipe each time, copy it and store it in the plastic sleeve above the day it is used. It will not only be readily available but protected from splatters too.

Seasonal and Yearly Stuff

Every part of the country is different when it comes to organizing for the seasons. You probably have some more empty cards in your Flipper. Use them to put down things you want to do for winter, summer, spring, fall, or once a year. If you can put monthly cards in your Flipper, choose a month for these seasonal things and include the jobs there. This is the streamlined version of the Flipper, so only put down the bare necessities. Omit things like "Test the fuses in the fuse box," which I suppose is good to do if you still have a fuse box but is definitely not part of the streamlined version of the Flipper.

That's the Flipper! Adjust it to meet your own needs. You'll do just great, I'm sure. Remember, the Flipper is your friendly helper, not your boss. It remembers for you and takes away the pressure of daily decision making. Visit it regularly. Like any good friend, it can help you a lot, if you let it.

15

The Mount Vesuvius Method

*We get rid of clutter in order to make
room for personal fulfillment.*

This is a powerful approach to big, bad jobs. Unless you have a
really tough situation, don't read this chapter. If you have a disaster that the Mount Vernon Method can't handle, this chapter
will be worth the price of the book.

My husband, a practicing, quick-witted Messie, was talking
to another Messie about the problems of getting things under
control.

"Do you use the Mount Vernon Method?" she asked.

"The Mount Vernon Method! I need the Mount Vesuvius
Method!" he replied.

They both laughed, instinctively understanding, in a way that
only a true Messie can, that he was saying the Mount Vernon
Method was too advanced for his situation. Before he could
even begin the Mount Vernon Method, he needed volcanic
power like that found in Mount Vesuvius. Sometimes the orderly, systematic approach of the Mount Vernon Method, which

has made it the reliable backbone of Messies Anonymous, is not the appropriate method for emergency situations.

In a "junk room" in which clothes, books, papers, and other assorted stuff cover the floor and all other surfaces, it is impossible to work around the room in a systematic way as required in the Mount Vernon Method. A basement, a garage, a utility room, or even a utility closet may need an alternative approach: the Mount Vesuvius Method. Sometimes the whole house needs this approach.

Mount Vesuvius is the only active volcano in Europe. For centuries it has been erupting, periodically pouring out smoke and lava on the countryside around it. It is the power of Mount Vesuvius that attracts us Messies to it as an inspiration for cleanup. Here are the steps for the Mount Vesuvius Method.

1. Have a Burning Determination

Volcanoes are formed when the hot molten rock under the earth comes under great pressure from the weight of the solid rock around it, which forces it violently up through a crack in the earth. That is exactly what happens to us Messies when we live in extreme clutter. One day the pressure of the weight of all this stuff becomes too great. Sometimes this pressure is caused by company coming, an awakening to how destructive this way of life is to us, or some other paradigm shift in our thinking. Like Vesuvius, we can't take the pressure anymore. We explode with energy and resolve to make a change. That is the beginning.

2. Use the Force of the Eruption

Volcanoes spew out their internal debris from a vent in the center. If you can get into the room, plant yourself on a spot in the center of the room. If not, symbolically center yourself for action. Inside your mind, whether you are aware of it or not, you already have an idea of what categories of things are in the room, although you can expect some surprises.

Buy the white boxes I mentioned in chapter 13. Don't buy too few. Attach typing-size papers with large, bold hand-lettered signs telling what is to fit into the boxes.

Designate a spot around the room for each category, or outside the room if you must. Toys, here. Clothes, there. Books, here. Papers, over there. Giveaway and trash right here beside me. And on it goes. Now just wade in. In volcano fashion, throw the various items into their designated boxes.

Because you honor them so much, you will probably want to walk the books into their place instead of throwing them. At your feet, have a treasure box for those things you come across that you have not seen in five years and are really valuable to you such as jewelry, money, photos, and the like.

When a box is full, put the top on. Place those filled boxes near where the items will be finally stored.

3. Don't Scrutinize

When dealing with paper put whole piles of unexamined papers into boxes and label where each pile of papers came from on the outside of the box in pencil or pen. When writing on the box itself, don't make it in large marker letters. That will look ugly when we store the boxes.

If you wish, divide the layers with colored papers and indicate where each layer came from. You need to feel some comfort that you will be able to locate the papers you are putting away. For example, write: *Papers—right front corner of dining room table.*

141

The main point of this method is not to simplify but to sort and store—to get them into categorized boxes. If you come across obvious and blatant junk, get rid of it. But don't examine piles and try to make decisions as you go. Just get the stuff off the floor, table, etc. and into the boxes as quickly as possible.

Putting things into boxes without making decisions about what to keep and what to get rid of may make you feel uncomfortable. You will feel better if you remember that this is the Mount Vesuvius Method. We are dealing with a disaster here. There is not enough time to "do it right."

When they are filled, put the tops on and stack the boxes up the side of a wall, hopefully outside the room you are clearing, with the labeled side out so you can have confidence you can locate anything you may need. Later you may go back and weed out the things you do not want to keep, one box at a time. At that point, you may wish to set up storage areas for the various items you wish to keep.

To review, when you are finished (now those are four little words with a lot of power):

- close the boxes
- take the giveaway boxes to the car immediately for early delivery to the closest charity
- toss the throwaway stuff immediately
- label the contents of the boxes you want to keep on the side of the boxes and take them out of the room to the back porch, covered patio, a friend's warehouse or garage, or somewhere else

Check chapter 13 for more information about how to label the boxes for retrieval of the items in the box.

Just get them out of the way so you can have your room back! Later you can deal with them, but for now use that short-lived but effective, explosive power to get the room uncluttered and clear.

Warnings

Before you begin, determine to finish some portion of the job completely before quitting. It is too easy to get started with a bang and run out of steam in the middle, leaving the room more chaotic than before because the job is half done. Maybe you will choose just to do all of the books or all of the clothes. Or perhaps you will choose just to do one quadrant of the offending room at a time. But be sure to finish, box, and get rid of the boxed clutter from whatever part you choose to do. Don't bite off more than you can chew. Make each session a self-contained activity that has a definite feeling of completion so you can feel good about having reached your goal. Nothing is more discouraging than wearing yourself out doing a Herculean job of organizing and then looking around and seeing that it looks pretty much the same except the stuff is just in different piles.

One woman doing this kind of job had a truck parked outside her house into which she loaded the stuff as she ejected it from her life. But before she could get the junk to the dump, or wherever, the owner of the truck came to get it back and she had to unload it back into her house. Plan ahead. Don't get caught short.

Another word of warning: Don't let the clutter spill out into the other parts of the house. In your zeal to get your targeted area clean, you may be tempted to put the stuff in the living room or some other inappropriate place "just for now until I get back to it." Flee from that temptation! Don't entertain the

143

idea even for a second. You will be compounding the problem. Do the hard thing. Follow through completely on each activity. After each session, the house should look better, not worse, while waiting to be better.

One more word of warning: Recognize the limits of this method. The Mount Vesuvius Method is very powerful. It *will* enable you to clear up large quantities of clutter. But it cannot solve the problem of super, extreme quantities of stuff.

There comes a point when the Messie's collection of clutter becomes so extensive that the best approach is to leave the house altogether and ask for help to devise a method of handling what is in there.

Sara had such a situation. She left her house and moved to an assisted living facility, taking only one trinket with her from her giant "collections." Sara was very happy to be free of the burden of her possessions.

She asked two of her longtime, very good friends to dispose of the items in her house. Throughout their friendship, they had never been inside Sara's house. Clearing out the stuff was a formidable task, indeed. Stuff was everywhere, crowding rooms and blocking doors. But Sara's friends did it.

Sara died happy in the end. She had been able to let go in the struggle with the maintenance of her stuff. All the clutter had been taken care of.

This story has a happy ending. Often, however, those who should leave their homes and let someone else take care of their things are not willing to do that. Well-meaning family and friends sometimes take it upon themselves to take over in these desperate situations. If not done with the person's permission and cooperation, this can cause serious consequences both to the person and the relationships. On the other hand, some situations are so dangerous that outside intervention seems to be unavoidable. Seek professional advice on how to proceed.

In the summer of AD 63, Mount Vesuvius erupted suddenly and buried the city of Pompeii with 20,000 occupants and all of their belongings. Its location was lost. About 1,800 years later archaeologists found and excavated it. Under all of the silt was a beautiful city full of paintings, intricate tile work, delicate jewelry, and pottery, among other things. If we refocus our metaphor, we can see that our room is like Pompeii. Under all of the debris are wonderful possibilities for beauty. We are the archaeologists, and as we do the job we too will be delighted with what we find.

Keep in mind your goal as you dig for that beauty. Get a clear picture, either out of a magazine or your imagination, of what your dream room would be. The energy from that vision will add fuel to your efforts. Make your desire something worth all of this effort, something big and splendid enough to inspire you. Organizing and beautifying your house can be a significant addition to your life. It's not just space. It is a part of your support system and an extension of yourself. If you have a vision of what that can mean to you, don't stop until your dream comes true. Don't settle for less!

16

Keeping Up with the Info Flow

*If you have made up your mind that you
can do something, you're absolutely right.*

The chief problem in today's world is not information itself but the constant flow of information into our lives. Most of us Messies love information and let it flow unabated into our lives.

- We love it in the newspapers, magazines, on radio, on TV, and any other way it may be funneled into our lives.
- We even love receipts because they give us information about what we bought and when. They are moments of our lives crystallized on paper.
- We love old ads because they tell us how much things used to cost.
- We love books, especially hardbound ones, which are a cut above the paperbacks even if they are the same books. Once we read them, we have mixed our thoughts with them so they are even more valuable.

- We love what the mail carrier brings to our doors and what somebody sticks under our windshields while we are at the mall.
- We love computers with their extensive information holders like CD encyclopedias. Even if we don't go looking for it, our friends and others forward information on our email. They send jokes, warnings, opportunities, inquiries. We can tap the motherlode of information, the internet. Using that little mouse and following the appropriate paths, we can find and print out reams of knowledge.

We are like hungry whales of inquiry gulping up tons of rich information plankton in a very big sea. Messies who are infoholics never seem to get full.

No generation previous to ours has had such access to so much. There has always been more information available than any one person could deal with. However, this is the first generation that has had to grapple with information overload from so many sources. We need to build boundaries to protect ourselves from information we don't want and set up ways of first limiting and then handling information we may want.

Being curious, exuberant, vivacious people, Messies have special problems with setting these boundaries. Being disorganized people, we have trouble knowing what to do with the stuff we decide to keep.

Barney Fife used to tell Andy Griffith on *The Andy Griffith Show*, "Nip it! Nip it in the bud!" when confronting misbehavior he was afraid would burst into a crime wave. That needs to be our motto.

Please understand that it is not the papers that the information comes on that is the chief problem, though the paper is an additional complication. It is the information itself.

Some Suggestions on How to Nip It!

Decide now what your limitations are. Here are mine. You may disagree with them entirely. Decide what you are going to do for yourself.

Nonpaper Information

I seldom watch TV news shows or listen to radio news stations, and yet I find that I know what is going on. Anyone with any access to the outside world cannot avoid the basics of news coverage. Obviously I miss specifics and the background of news stories to a large extent. That is exactly what I want to do. I don't want to know the exquisite detail of the world's woes (or joys, for that matter).

Do I miss any important information? I'm sure I do. And I am very willing to—in exchange for the freedom to concentrate on dealing with bad news and creating good news in my own personal life.

Newspapers and Magazines

I canceled all my newspaper and magazine subscriptions. I can hardly believe I did that. I believe in the press; I just can't handle it on a daily basis.

I do get two small writing magazines. Occasionally I buy a newspaper or magazine that contains something I am interested in.

Has my life been negatively impacted? I am sure that I have missed crumbs of information that would have benefited me in the mountain of knowledge I could have accessed, but nobody ever says to me, "You didn't know such-and-such has happened?" Somehow it all gets to me.

The freedom from knowing and caring about vast amounts of alluring stuff has positively impacted my life. The magazines I peruse at the hairdresser's and in the dentist's office are enough for me.

Unrequested Papers

Flyers, offers, and junk mail in general goes right to the trash unread. I am embarrassed to tell you that lately I have even littered the ground at malls with flyers, hoping the mall managers will forbid distribution if they see the littered parking lot. I feel no responsibility to read, handle, or dispose of any paper I did not request. People who push paper on us are abusing us. There is no need for us to honor their mistreatment by processing their information in any way.

My approach may be surprising, but it is necessary for me. I cannot afford the mental energy of carrying around all kinds of interesting information that is of no direct use to me. I cannot afford to spend emotional energy caring about situations I can do nothing about when I have more things to care for in my immediate life than I can handle now. I cannot be distracted by the shocking stories and urgent warnings so popular with the media if I am going to be fully aware of the areas that need my concern in my own life and the lives of my family and friends.

Do I selfishly neglect those in need? Some areas outside my immediate living space do need my care and concern. I inform myself and reach out to the needy through chosen charities I am particularly interested in and through my church. By weeding out the multitude of appeals, I can concentrate on a few in which I can make a difference.

Handling Chosen Information

Once you have put the brakes on the information you want, you need to keep it in such a way that it is out of the way when you don't want it and easily accessed when you do.

Everybody loses information now and again. But we want to set up systems that will avoid that as much as possible. Here are several tried-and-true classic organizational systems:

1. Information box
2. Telephone/Address book
3. Notebook, planner, or organizer
4. Computer

1. Information Box

The box is a wooden, metal, or plastic container that holds index cards. Such "recipe" boxes are sold in drugstores, grocery stores, and department stores; they can also be purchased in stationery stores, where they are called index boxes.

I've found that three-by-five-inch file cards work best for me. Along with your box you will need to purchase one or two packages of file cards, some three-by-five-inch dividers labeled A to Z, and some dividers that you can label yourself. These dividers will separate the contents of the box into several main sections.

Obviously, the A–Z part of the box will become your telephone and address file. You may find it useful to divide this file into two parts, personal and business, in the same way the telephone company divides its phone book. You may wish to divide the business section into categories such as doctors, finances, stores, etc. If you only have a few names to keep up with, you may want to do it alphabetically by name.

Any number you call or address you use should be put into the file in the box. Addresses put in books are hard to maintain. The books get full and the addresses need changing, so we cross out one address and put another over it. This looks messy and the book becomes obsolete because of the changes. The box file solves that problem because if a change needs to be made, the original card can be thrown away and a new card put in.

The box is also better than an address book because there is room to make notes. Let us say you have a friend from college whom you never see but with whom you correspond at Christmas. You get a birth announcement from her. Write down on the card the name of the new baby and the date of birth. Then when you send your card you can write, "How is little Helen? Kids are so cute at two." You can also make notes about friends' likes and dislikes in food, how their coffee is taken, and so on. They will be pleased you remembered.

BUSINESS RECORDS

If it is a business call you make, you can make notes for that too. If you have a plumber come, make a note about what he did and the date. Then if the same thing breaks down again, you can tell him when he was there previously and what he did. Keep records of car repairs and expenses under C for car.

Making notes in the box is valuable for keeping track of orders you place. If you buy something by mail, write down the name and address of the company and the date you ordered it. If it does not come within a reasonable length of time, you can write, telling them how long it has been since your order. Put down the date of the inquiry letter on your card as well. In this way we can keep our lives under control by having necessary information readily available.

NEWSPAPER CLIPPINGS

The A to Z file can also take the place of a newspaper clippings pile. Suppose you have an interest in restaurants and your local paper carries regular reviews of restaurants. Instead of cutting out the article, transfer the information to a card and file it under R for restaurants.

If someone recommends a book to you, write it on a card and file it under B for book. You'll have all the information summarized and at hand when you want it.

If you have some short-term miscellaneous information you want to keep, put it on a piece of scrap paper and file it in the box. Throw the paper away when you have finished with it.

A lot of those scrap pieces of paper are getting lost because they don't have any home to go to. Make your box their home.

MONTHLY ACTIVITIES

The monthly activities part of the box is used to store reminders of activities that are done only seasonally or yearly. If you use a Flipper which has monthly cards, you may wish to omit this monthly section of the box and use the Flipper instead.

Wherever you decide to place your monthly reminders, check your monthly card at the beginning of each month. Say you wish to turn your mattress four times a year. On the cards for January, April, July, and October put "Turn mattress in master bedroom."

You will also wish to list birthdays and anniversaries behind the month in which they occur so you can send a card or make a call for the special occasion. If the event is on November 1, put the notice in October.

Once you start using the box you'll think of lots and lots of wonderful uses for it.

Special Interests

The special interests part of the box is for keeping information that is unique to your home and family. There are four or five blank dividers for that purpose. I use mine for storage information, like where I stored the Christmas, Halloween, or seasonal things. I use it for notes on a real estate course I took. I use it for records of special days, things like who came to the house on Christmas last year, what we had for dinner, and what gifts were received. I am sentimental, I guess. It makes me feel good to know one card per holiday has those memories safely preserved.

One person I know has a divider labeled "health." In that section she has a separate card for each member of her family. She records the dates of immunizations, surgeries, and so on, and details information about allergies.

In a section on "finances" she keeps cards that contain all the insurance policy numbers for life, health, car, and fire insurance. She also records checking and savings account numbers and credit card information. Because her savings passbooks are exactly three-by-five, she files them in this section. In the event of an emergency she has all her vital information at her fingertips.

Storage

You will need to keep up with storage items which you have placed in boxes. List on the box, perhaps using a three-by-five card taped to the side, what is in it. Make a corresponding card with the same information on it. Then number the box and the card to match. Store the card in the section called "storage." Put the boxes in numerical order wherever you are going to be storing them.

Now when you need holiday items, seasonal clothes, and the like, you can put your finger right on them.

2. Telephone-Address Book

Nothing quite substitutes for the old-fashioned little black book as mentioned earlier. The chief problem is that they get filled up and out-of-date after a while and need to be redone. They are also easily lost if you are not zealous about keeping them in the same location. The advantage is that you can carry them easily with you and, with a flip of a page, the information is very accessible.

At the bedroom phone I have a small telephone book (like a little black book but mine is brightly colored) with most of the personal phone numbers I need.

If you have a phone with memory into which numbers can be programmed, take the time and effort to figure out how to put them in and do it right away.

If it is not unsightly, put frequently used numbers on a three-by-five-inch card on the wall or table beside the telephone so you won't have to consult the book for those numbers.

Some computer programs print out addresses on pages of many sizes; the print sizes are designed to fit the most popular personal organizers. This printout capability solves the problem of having to recopy the address book.

Simple handheld electronic organizers often function as telephone and address books. They are no bigger than a traditional little black book and don't need to be recopied. Some of them work in conjunction with your regular desktop computer, sharing information. If you are computer literate, all of this is very empowering and convenient.

The handheld organizers do have the disadvantage that, being electronic, they can go down, or you can drop them and lose your info. Of course, if you have backed them up on the computer, you have not lost your information.

Keep a phone memo book that makes a carbonless copy with a ballpoint pen beside the phone at all times. Keep all phone messages in this book. Write the dates on the outside edge of the pages. At important messages you may wish to locate later, put a small sticky note with a written notation. This will be a wonderful organizational gift you give yourself.

3. Notebook, Planner, or Organizer

Everybody needs a notebook of some kind to carry around in order to hold information. Otherwise we end up making notes on little pieces of paper and leaving a trail of lost scraps of information behind us. That's okay if you are lost in the woods and need to follow your trail back out. If you're not lost in the woods, this method is pretty useless.

In a notebook you can list things to do when you are out, things to buy, important sizes of clothes, or the title of a book that has been recommended by a friend. Some are designed to carry much more. In other words, it is a memory book.

There are basically three choices you can make.

NOTEBOOK

The simplest system is a cheap little spiral-bound notebook that slips easily into a purse, combined with a thin month-at-a-glance calendar. They are available in almost any store that sells paper products for school or office. The advantages are that it is simple to use and easy to keep up with.

PLANNER

The next step up is called a planner. It is a larger and more extensive information keeper than the little notebook. It usually has a week-at-a-glance calendar and a spot for a to-do list. The planner is available in office supply stores and sometimes in other stores, especially around the new year.

ORGANIZER

By far the most extensive notebook is the organizer. It is very comprehensive. Some people say it is like an office in a notebook. Others say they carry their entire lives in their organizer. Some manufacturers give courses and provide support in the use of these organizers. The disadvantages for those of us who are absentminded are that it is complex to use and you must carry it with you similar to the way you carry a purse. Lose it and you are dead in the water.

The truth about whatever we Messies decide to use is that we like to switch around a lot. Our perfectionism leads us to hunt for something better. We will decide on a wonderful new system with a zipper and leather binding at the beginning of the year. Somewhere about May, we will notice a flowered cloth binder that appeals to us and switch to that. Somehow, we slowly stop using that one so we decide on a "better" system of another kind.

We like a variety of systems and are unlikely to stick to one over a long period. We get bored easily. Of course, it would be better if we found one great system and consistently used it. Since we might not do that, we need to be alert to making as seamless a transition from one system to another as possible.

4. Computer

Many people, even those who are very computer literate, don't use their computers to organize their lives. If you think you might want to use the computer for your addresses, calendar, to-do list, etc., you have a very powerful tool at your command. If you are not at all interested at this time, just skip the next few paragraphs. But keep your mind open to the possibilities in the future.

ADDRESSES AND PHONE NUMBERS

Computers are great for keeping address information. Using a program that has a spreadsheet and prints labels makes the addresses you have very versatile.

But computers can crash. It's important to back up your information. Keep that information on a hard copy or on your handheld electronic organizer in case it crashes and because it is not always convenient to wait for the computer to boot up.

TO-DO LISTS, CALENDARS, AND MISCELLANEOUS INFORMATION

These can be stored and retrieved very easily in a computer. They can be transferred to the latest handheld organizer. The computer and handheld organizer can transfer information back and forth and save their owner lots of time. The handheld organizer has information easily accessible and does not have to be booted up. It is as small as a small notebook so it can easily be carried in a pocket or purse.

One of the best ideas I ever received is one I picked up from a professor of pharmacology at the University of Miami Medical School who is a member of my local writers' association. As we talked across the table at an awards banquet, he mentioned keeping a running journal on his computer. A kind of "boing" went off in my brain. It seemed so clear. So I went home and, using my word processing program, began noting things I did each day. If I made a call, I noted the call and the number that I called. I always try to include a key word in case I can't recall the details or the name. For example: "Called plumber, Jim Brown, at 721-2000. Appt. set for Tues., Feb. 3." That way, if I needed to follow up later, all I had to do was open my Macintosh FIND command (in most PC programs it's called search/change; Windows 95 calls it FIND), type the name of what I was looking for in the computer, and press the FIND button.

An unexpected advantage of this idea was that it enabled me to throw away many papers I was keeping just for a scrap of information on them: an address, a recommendation of a good book, an ad for an item. I kept all of these on the papers they came on. When I put the information in my computer journal, I threw away the paper.

Now the information is easily accessible, unlike when it was floating around on a piece of paper. Fewer piles to worry about.

Piling and Filing

Many creative types distrust filing cabinets and the whole filing concept. So they drop things in piles and rely on their already overstuffed memories to recall where to retrieve them. They do a lot of shuffling and looking, handling the same papers over and over again. Frustration builds and productivity plummets.

Piling is not efficient. What system will work for the creative personality who fears the filing process? I've got good news. One kind of paper doesn't need filing.

It is the junk paper that plagues modern society. I hope you have strengthened your resolve to eliminate these from your life quickly. If your trash can is small, buy a large one, or recycle. The larger the trash can or recycle bin, the easier it will be for you to throw away junk papers. On the computer, use the delete button freely. Email and old documents may not have any actual weight, but they weigh down the mind and clutter the spirit.

1. Create a Vertical To-Do Pile

One of the worst problems anyone grapples with is the problem of piles of papers that are waiting for some kind of action. Papers such as warranties to fill out, a numbered receipt from a rapid mail service that you need to save for tracking, a story a friend wants you to critique are all waiting for action. So where do they go?

They used to go in a great big pile. Vow not to do that anymore. Now you will put them in your vertical to-do pile. You will take your horizontal pile and make it accessible by making it vertical.

I learned this valuable system from Marsha Sims, a friend and professional organizer in Miami. She deserves credit from all the paper-weary world for spotlighting and refining this system. It has been the best thing I have found since the automatic dialing buttons on the phone. I have added a few of my personal touches to the idea.

- At any office supply store get a file crate of some kind that will hold hanging files. Each of the hanging files will contain a paper that would otherwise have been put in a pile. Don't worry about the colors of the hanging files. This method is a casual deal and is not meant to be pretty or permanent.
- Put the paper into the hanging file.

- Get a small sticky note (like a Post-it brand), turn it upside down so that the sticky part is on the bottom of the back side, and write at the top of that sticky note what needs to be done with the paper at some time in the future. (Throw away the plastic label holders that come with the hanging files.) Start each notation with a verb. Be specific about the action: "Fill in this survey," or "Order this book."
- Slap that sticky note on the file that has the paper in it. Make the verb message stand up above the top of the folder like the plastic label holder would have done.
- Now slam-dunk that hanging file into the file container. There! No more pile!

Following are some examples. Notice all of them begin with action verbs.

Pizza Coupons—*Use* pizza coupons by 4–12.

Promotional for a conference in Dallas—Decide about trip to Dallas.

Sketch you have for an idea for a board game—Call library for info about game producers.

College catalog—Sign up for gardening course.

Receipt for cleaning—Pick up cleaning.

Paint swatches—Paint the living room.

If you kept just a few items you could store them in a little drawer just like a lot of people do, but people who are disorganized keep more papers than most people for two reasons: (1) Because we need more time to make up our minds, and (2) we have more creative ideas to follow through on than most people.

You may never do some of these activities. Whether you choose to do them is irrelevant. These are not commands. They are just action steps if you should decide to pursue these projects.

You may very well let the pizza coupons expire and never sign up for the gardening course. I have a package of seeds I have been storing in my vertical to-do file (under "Plant these seeds") for a couple of years. I expect they are too old to germinate now. That's fine. I chose not to plant them. But at least it was a choice, not a default I had to make because I didn't know where the seeds were.

I have divided my hanging pile into four large groups by stapling index cards with labels onto hanging files. My groups are: Give (papers for other people), Write, Do, Wait. You may want to divide your items into some larger categories to meet your needs. If I paid the bills in my house, I would have a group for bills.

Notice that all of these activities have papers connected with the activity. They are not paperless to-do activities such as "Call Mother on her birthday." Only papers or other things like a package of seeds that would end up in a pile otherwise go in the vertical to-do pile.

Warning: Don't start being perfectionistic about this pile and trying to alphabetize it or color code it. You may think of some improvement that will work for you, but be careful of getting too perfect. The reason it works is because it is designed to stay informal and random, like a pile.

2. Set Up a Formal File

Messies both love and hate files. Mostly we are afraid of them. They require too many decisions about where to put things, and they require too much memory about where to find the things we have put in there.

Omit filing as many papers as you can. If you have piles and piles sitting around, don't try to file them. Start from where you are today and file only the new papers that come in. You may need to file some of the old papers such as birth certificates and other important papers. For the most part, use the Mount Vesuvius Method to box the other papers you decide to keep. You will label those boxes so they become archival files of a sort.

Materials

First of all, obtain the materials you need. Use a hanging file system. Buy the metal frame and the file folders that have hooks on the ends that hang over the frame, like the system made by Pendaflex. Use this type exclusively. Don't use internal folders inside the hanging files any more than you have to. They are just unnecessary clutter. Some file cabinets have a frame for hanging the file folders. You will need to buy frames for the ones that do not. Legal size folders are easier to use when filing and retrieving papers, so if you need to buy a new cabinet, get a lateral file or one that accommodates legal folders.

Buy the best quality filing cabinet you can. Nothing discourages filing like wrestling with a sticking drawer. Make sure they pull out the whole twenty-six or twenty-seven inches and don't stop partway.

Categories

Decide what categories you need. Here are two systems suggested by professional organizers, many of whose clients think like we do.

System 1. Judith Kolberg, a professional organizer who founded Fileheads in Atlanta, recently organized a home office using the following groupings. They will work for homes as well: Past (bills, old taxes, archive documents, and so forth), Present (bills currently due, correspondence, calls to make, etc.), Future (long-term projects).

Judith urges "clinging to the future" instead of the past as a way to move forward into a productive and happy life.

System 2. Marsha Sims of Sort-It-Out Professional Organizers in Miami uses a five-category system since five is the number of colors in standard assorted hanging file folder packages. Her categories are People, Places and Things, Finances, Ideas and Interests, Work.

Choose categories that make sense to you. Since making category decisions is hard for some of us, you might want to use one of these two systems. Flip a coin if you get stuck on which one. Later you will understand why it doesn't really matter very much how you categorize. This system is foolproof, even for folks who have trouble grouping things or knowing how to label.

Once you have decided on the categories, divide the papers up into those categories and put them into hanging file folders. Always file new papers to the front of the folder facing in one direction. Use one color per category. For example: People—blue file folders; Finances—green file folders; Work—yellow file folders.

Use self-stick removable notes such as the ones you use in the vertical to-do file as temporary tabs when first setting up your file. The removable notes give you easy flexibility to change your mind and reshuffle your system. Put in the more permanent plastic tabs later.

Alphabetize the file folders within the color-coded groups. For instance, in the People category you will put Alan, Betty, Clarissa, David, or whatever so that you can find them easily.

List the categories in the file drawer on the outside of the file drawer. Most file drawers have pockets to hold this information. If not, affix a card with tape. Don't let a file cabinet drawer become more than three-quarters full. If there is any resistance when you start to file because it is too tight, you will start piling instead.

Let's be realistic. Some things are not that easy to categorize. Car insurance can go under auto, car, insurance, or some other creative idea. If you put it under car, that is fine. If you put it under insurance, that is fine too. Relax. Just do it. It will work out as the system progresses.

THE COMPREHENSIVE MASTER LIST

Using a simple word processing program, make a comprehensive master file list on the computer. Going drawer by drawer, type in every individual file folder you have in the filing cabinet. If you do this on the computer, you can add to the list easily each time you insert a new folder.

Indicate which drawer the files are in (put a number on the outside of each drawer). Some folders, like *car insurance*, may need another key word like *auto* just in case you decide to look for it using the word *auto*.

To make my list, I sat at my computer and had a friend call out the heading at the top of each hanging file folder. Obviously, having help allowed me to avoid hopping up and down to look. I had already grouped and alphabetized the headings. It did not take as much time as you might think. She read and I typed quickly. Each new heading was placed on a line below the previous one.

Now the computer has all the information about what is in my file and will "remember." I don't even have to try.

SIXTY-SECOND RETRIEVAL

Now here is the payoff for all of this work.

To test this system for you, I decided to get out the house insurance policy. Not something I get every day.

Did I strive to remember where the policy might be in my file? Not for a second. This system is designed to circumvent use of human memory entirely. After I opened my "master file list" document, I activated my FIND command on my Mac. I asked the computer to locate *insurance*. There were four insurances, one of which was the house insurance. The computer directed me to the correct drawer. I could have looked under house and found it just as easily.

It took less than sixty seconds. But the real value of the system is that I did not get that panicky feeling I used to get when approaching my file because I knew that the computer would tell me just where to go.

If you don't use a computer, you can make and use lists manually, but nothing beats using that majestic FIND command.

If all of this sounds complex, begin one or two steps to start. Wander around the office supply store or catalog with this information in hand. It will all begin to come together.

I have written about this system in some detail so that it will be very clear. I didn't want to overlook any point that might stump you along the way and cause you to stop. I hope I have not made it sound complicated. It is not. Go step-by-step. Then be sure to keep going until you incorporate all of the steps into your system.

In the end, this system will give you power and uncomplicate your life to such an extent that you will have on your screen saver, "Thank you forever, Sandra Felton!" or something like that. My biggest thank-you will be for you to be stress free and productive while using your file.

17
Closets

Order is a lonely nymph.

Samuel Johnson

Don't you think it's wonderful when you go to see a Cleanie and she says, "Have you seen my house? Would you like a tour?" Then she parades you all through, even into the bedroom and opens the closet door! "This is my closet," she says. Wow! She even takes pride in her closets. And the closets reflect it.

Let me digress to say that the reason Cleanies show you around the house is because they consider the house an art form, and they work at each part of their homes in the same way in which an artist paints different areas of canvas. As you work on the house, think that there might be a time when you will want to show people around your house with pride or at least take them to the bedroom closet to show them a new dress you have bought with the confidence that you will be proud of your closet.

Clothes Closets

What is the closet problem? Most closets are too small. However, if you look at your closet you will see a lot of wasted space, usually below the clothes and above the clothes rod.

The logical solution is to put two bars one above the other, thus making better use of more space in the closet. To put in two bars, the top bar needs to be raised. Carmen, one of my Cleanie friends, did this by taking out all the wood shelves and bars and replacing them with plastic-coated, ventilated wire shelving. There are three advantages to this type of shelving. One is that you can see what is on the high shelf more easily through the spaces between the wire. Another is that it requires less dusting since there is no solid shelf. A third is that if you wish to buy shelving without a bar, the shelf holds the clothes hangers apart evenly. JC Penney and home improvement stores have a whole section on this type of closet.

There are closet companies that will do this for you if you cross their palms with silver. Look under "closets" in the Yellow Pages.

Now suppose you say, "That's too big a job for right now. What can I do with my closet the way it is?" Let me tell you my situation. If it requires a hammer and nails and takes more than five minutes to do, I don't do it. My husband and I are not handy with building things and the few occasions when I have had someone do it for me have been unsatisfactory. So I look for easy-to-install ready-builts. In this case, add another shelf to the top of the closet with boxes and a board or one you find in a store in order to make use of the empty space up there. Of course, that shelf will be pretty much out of reach so you should use it to store only seldom-used things. The unused space at the bottom of the closet can be utilized as a basket storage system. Look in department stores for suitable baskets.

An easy-to-install lower bar can be hung from the one above by two chains. A PVC pipe hung with a rope works great. Look in catalogs for this. A low bar in the closet helps the children get in the hanging-up habit, too.

Now comes what I think is the most chronic problem of the clothes closet—shoes. If they are left on the floor, even if they are on a wire floor rack with a hump for each shoe, they are unsightly, gather dust, and make it impossible to dust easily. There are several solutions. The one I am using now is the one Carmen suggested. I keep the boxes the shoes come in and stack them with the shoes in the bottom of the closet. I write in large letters on the outside of the box a description of the shoes. When I get my shoes out I leave the top ajar and the box pulled out a little so I will know where to put them back. It works well for me.

There are other good methods. The point is, don't let the shoes make your closet a mess. The back of the closet door is invaluable for storage of shoes, belts, ties, and some jewelry. If you make your closet a project (after you have finished the Mount Vernon Method, of course), go to the library or the bookstore and check out the newest closet upgrade ideas.

An important element of clothing storage that is often overlooked is the clothes hanger. Get rid of the wire hangers; buy plastic tubular ones instead. And have enough hangers. One reason people don't hang up their clothes is because it is so hard. Sometimes there aren't enough hangers. The wire coat hangers hook over each other, making them hard to take out. Frequently the wire hangers with the round cardboard tube from dry cleaners break in the middle of the tube, which discourages hanging up pants. You can pick up the plastic tubular hangers at many dollar-day sales, or buy a few each time you go to the store.

I suggest you paint your closet white and keep it that way so you won't have to repaint it each time you paint the bedroom. Buy one color of hangers; brown is good because it is stylish and somewhat neutral. Can you envision that beautiful neat closet with the white walls and brown hangers? Looks good, doesn't it?

The best color-coding application I have ever made is with my clothing. I divided my clothes into four groups: slacks, blouses, two-piece outfits, and dresses. In each group I arranged the clothes from light to dark like an artist's palette. This did wonders. Previously, I could not tell whether the pair of slacks I was looking for was out of the closet or lost under something in the closet. Now I know that if my black slacks are not right at the end of the slacks section, they are not in the closet. This trick also helps me to see what clothes I have and how I can mix and match them. I highly recommend it to you.

In order to keep the clothes in their "official" positions, use a round "doughnut," similar to the kind used in stores to divide sizes of clothing. Make your own from heavy tagboard. (There is a pattern, if you need it, in the free introductory Messies Anonymous information or they are available in plastic from us as well. Check out www.messies.com.)

And then of course, there is the problem of too many clothes in the closet, which makes getting something in or out a tug-of-war. Perhaps in no other area are we more tempted to keep unused things than with clothes. We have things too big or too small in case we gain or lose weight. We have things that are good but that we never wear because we don't like them. But they are good; that is, they fit and the buttons are on. So we have to keep them—especially if we paid a lot for them. We keep out-of-style things we used to love, just in case the style returns. It seldom does, and never in the same way. Sometimes we keep a dress that is out of style because the skirt could be made into something nice. We never get to that project; but if we ever do, we will have that wonderful dress to work with.

The worst reason to keep clothes cluttering up our closets is that we are keeping them in case someone else would like them. Sometimes we don't have a specific person in mind, so we keep them until we locate somebody who would profit by our generosity. Being perfectionists, we have to make sure it is just the perfect person. So we put the clothes aside until we get around to sending them to cousin Mary's boy. He'll probably have a son of his own before we get them in the mail!

Listen, let's quit dreaming. We are not going to do the alterations. We are not going to gain or lose weight while the style is still in. If we do, we can reward ourselves with new clothes. Don't wait for the perfect person to wear the outfit you are saving. Give it to the Salvation Army. Let them find the perfect person.

Utility Closet

Tangled extension cords, lightbulbs, picture-hanging kits—these are hard-to-store things that go into a utility closet or wherever you store miscellaneous items that are a part of modern living. I have a super idea for solving that problem and I want to share it with you: open plastic baskets. They are wonderful. When I first cleaned out the utility closet I found that the items to be put away were falling into categories. So I bought plastic shoe boxes and later plastic baskets. On the outside I wrote the various categories and put the groups of items in them. My boxes include:

- Shoe things (polishes, laces, brushes)
- Electric repair stuff (light switch plates, wall plugs, etc.)
- Curtain hardware (hooks for curtains, plastic balls for the pull cords, curtain rod brackets)
- Tape, ribbon, and string
- Lightbulbs
- Soap, toothpaste, and emery boards

The category must be put on the front with a labeling gun or with tabs used for labeling in a filing system or with index cards marked with markers. (Messies Anonymous provides "official" cards with pictures on them. Pictures help the kids to know what's in the boxes.)

If you store mops or brooms in the utility closet, buy clamps and attach them to the wall. Awkward things like irons and ironing boards can be stored with special holders designed to keep them off the floor. Try to keep the floor as bare as possible. It's easier to keep clean that way and looks much neater.

> It's a little-known fact, but true,
> One I gladly pass on to you:
> Paper clips—scarce in any home—
> Have an inborn tendency to roam.
>
> But coat hangers hang till the end,
> Like crowded but genial friends.
> They tangle and trip, and ofttimes fall,
> But a coat hanger will always give you his all.
>
> While you slumber deep in the night,
> A paper clip starts on his flight.

As he moves, a wondrous change takes place:
He begins to grow a coat hanger's face!

And he hops into your closet with glee,
And crowds up by a coat hanger's knee,
For every paper clip has always known,
He'll be a coat hanger, when he's grown!

18

The Kitchen

*"If a guy has a messy apartment, he's just
your typical bachelor. But if a girl has a
messy apartment, she's branded a slob."*

CHARACTER IN *SNAGGED*, BY
CAROL HIGGINS CLARK

The general organization of the kitchen is very important. Using
the principles of storage, we know that things frequently used
should be stored in an easy-to-reach place and near the point
where they are needed. When I looked at my kitchen, I found
that my canned goods were near the dishwasher and my dishes
were by the stove. I was amazed that I had violated the logical rule of keeping things near where they were used. I had to
put the dishes closer to the dishwasher and the canned goods
closer to the stove. I wonder if the most obvious rules aren't
the most violated because we assume we will observe them
automatically?

When my children were in the home, I color coded my drinking glasses. Each person in the family had a different color. That way each person could use just one glass all day, and we could avoid the sink-full-of-glasses way of life.

If your people have a difficult time remembering which color is theirs, you can attach some meaning to the color. "Mary, your color is green because you are growing so fast." "June, you have the gold glass because you are so valuable and precious to us," and so forth.

But even with organizing the best I could, I came to the unhappy conclusion that most kitchens do not have enough storage space. One reason is that kitchens tend to collect too many unused items. Another reason is that there is a lot of unused space since the shelves are too far apart and several inches of space are wasted. Sometimes another shelf can be inserted to give more storage space. Wire rack shelves or wire hanging shelves can also be used to do the same thing.

The place under the sink is full of wasted space. It can be made useful by putting in shelves that avoid the pipe.

Hang-Up Tips

I am becoming more and more convinced that Cleanies do a lot of hanging up of things without even realizing it. They do it to keep surfaces clean—but it also helps when there are storage problems. Here are some quick hang-up tips for the kitchen:

- Use cup hooks or an accordion coatrack to hang up cups.
- Use hanging baskets to hang up fruits and veggies. We had limes, avocados, and oranges that took up valuable counter space until I bought a hanging basket.

- Hang knives on a magnetized knife rack. It frees drawer space and keeps them from nicking and dulling each other in the drawer.
- Hang up brooms and mops. This gets them off the floor where they tend to fall over and clutter things. It takes the pressure off the bristles, which can bend the broom and ruin it. You can buy holders for this purpose at the hardware store, or you can use a screw with an eye in the top of a wooden handle to hook on to a cup hook mounted on the wall.

The backs of doors are also very important for storage in the kitchen. You can put small wire shelves or racks for spices on the backs of doors. Racks made by Rubbermaid or other manufacturers for holding aluminum foil, bags, plastic wrap, soap and steel wool pads, and so on clear a lot of shelf space.

Cooking utensils can also be hung up, thus eliminating the clutter they cause in drawers. It is a good idea to hang measuring spoons on the back of a kitchen door on cup hooks. Hang pots on the wall, but be sure not to have so many things hanging around in the kitchen that it begins to look cluttered. Since shelf and drawer space are at a premium, hang or stand up anything that can be hung or stood up.

Shelves, Cabinets, and Countertops

In whatever way you arrange your shelves, you'll want to line them with an easy-to-clean liner.

Perhaps you will want to use adhesive-backed plastic paper like Con-Tact paper. It lasts for years. Drawers and cupboards are a pleasure to wipe out with a damp cloth.

If you've never used this kind of paper, you may find it a little difficult to handle at first. Cut it to the drawer or shelf size first, leaving the backing on. Tear off about a four-inch square piece of the backing in one corner. Being careful that the corner is turned up so it does not adhere, fit the sheet exactly. Then place that corner down. Now the paper won't slip.

Start at the opposite side and carefully peel off the backing. Be sure the sticky sides do not touch each other. Slowly slide your hand around so the paper spreads out in place. Now lift the other end up—including the stuck corner—and remove the rest of the backing. Smooth the paper in place. Many people have difficulty with their first attempts at laying adhesive-backed plastic paper, but with practice you can become adept.

If you have a kitchen cabinet with an open space above it, be sure to cover the upper surface. The top of the cabinet will become really dirty and greasy, but the covering will protect it and make it easier to clean.

Kitchen cabinets do get grimy. Clean painted ones with one cup of ammonia, a half cup of vinegar, and a fourth of a cup of baking soda in a bucket. Clean greasy wood-finished cabinets by rubbing them with fine steel wool and paint thinner. Work in one area at a time, using long strokes.

Butcher-block counters should be wiped with a cloth that has been wrung out with soapy water. Then dry the butcher block. Oil the top with mineral oil now and again. Do not use vegetable oil, or it will become rancid. If your counter is made of Formica, it will require very special treatment. Use baking soda to get stains off Formica countertops, and never use bleach or powdered cleansers.

Always check the manufacturer's suggestions for care. Homemade ideas are not as good.

Cabinet Organization

In order to know where things like canned and boxed goods are located in my kitchen cabinets, I label the shelf with words like tomato products, beans, baking supplies, etc. I fit smaller things into rectangular plastic baskets and label them supplements, condiments, etc.

These labels not only tell me where to find items, they tell me where to put them back. The labels help me maintain the system. The baskets keep things from moving around. As you know, labeling also guides my family so I don't have to be involved in finding things in the kitchen for them.

Appliances

Refrigerator Helps

In the refrigerator use plastic grids made for holding fruits and veggies up off the bottom of the crisper. They save the vegetables from spoiling and they save on cleaning. They are also useful in the bottom of a self-defrosting freezer. The grids keep the food from defrosting while the automatic freezer does.

Keep mildew at bay in the fridge by wiping the inside with vinegar. Don't forget to vacuum the refrigerator coils. Some are under the refrigerator and some are in the back of it. Keeping the coils dust free helps the refrigerator work with less effort, giving you better service and longer life for the appliance. This kind of job should be recorded on your Flipper on a month card. Remember also to clean the drip pan under the refrigerator regularly. Running it under hot water with a disinfectant, then spraying it with a mildew-resistant spray, will cut down on kitchen odors.

If you don't do this regularly (and most people probably don't), you can do it when you have to pull the refrigerator out to get the runaway gerbil. The point is, try not to let the job get away from you entirely.

As for organizing your refrigerator, perhaps the most innovative use for the labeling you have heard so much about is in the refrigerator. My family and I were always groping around in the back of the fridge for catsup or whatever while the food got cold on the table. We were forever buying something we thought we were out of only to find that it had been hiding behind something else. Part of the reason for all of this confusion is that we keep a bigger variety of food in the refrigerator than most people. Although all Messies need to modify the hoarding of too much stuff, keeping somewhat more than most people keep will probably continue to be to some extent part of the Messie lifestyle.

To solve the problem, I got plastic baskets and designated them for different categories of food such as dairy, leftovers, bread, meat, pickles, fruit, vegetables, etc. I label these baskets in the same way I label the storage closet. It works wonders! One reason for the success is that we can pull the basket out to see the things that might otherwise get lost in the rear of the refrigerator.

The Dishwasher

Automatic dishwashing powders can cause problems by stopping up the dishwasher with "gook." You can do several things about this. If it has been a problem for you, you might wish to try other brands until you find one that works.

In addition, set your water temperature to 140 degrees. (This setting will also prevent your clothes from becoming grayish in your washing machine.) It is also a good idea to turn on your hot water faucet for a little while to bring hot water into the pipes toward the dishwasher. Very hot water is needed to dissolve dishwashing powder and keep scum from forming. Another trick is to run a half cup to a full cup of white vinegar through the wash cycle periodically to keep scum and lime deposits from forming.

The Oven

Nobody seems to know how long it takes to clean the oven, but most Messies seem to think it is a very long job indeed. Actually, it is not. Then why does it seem so long? It's because it is distasteful. The fumes, the goo, having to bend over in an awkward way. It's a messy job, so we think it is a long job.

Frequently, the more distasteful a job is, the longer we think it will take. This may or may not be the case. The only way to tell how long a job really takes is to time it.

What is the result of this kind of thinking? It causes us to procrastinate. We dread doing jobs we perceive as too long. We need to face the fact that sometimes we are just kidding ourselves. Some jobs are not as long as we build them up to be in our minds.

Some jobs, however, are long and hard, and we just don't get to them because they overwhelm us. They sort of hover in the back of our minds, draining off energy as they hover there.

In these cases, we have to manage a breakthrough to get started. The best method is to approach the job from its blind side. Don't let the job know you are really going to tackle it.

Let's take oven cleaning as a for-instance. First, make a commitment to do the job. In some place away from the kitchen where the oven can't hear, tell somebody that you are going to clean the oven, or write it down as a commitment. Or both.

Second, get all the supplies in order. Buy an oven cleaner if you are out, rubber gloves, and sponges. Read the instructions on the oven cleaner spray can. Keep the materials close to the oven but out of sight, so the oven doesn't see them.

Fortunately, oven cleaning is generally done in two parts, so your approach is already planned. You are ready for the attack. Now that you have made the commitment and actually begun, your mind knows that you are serious about what you are doing and it will begin gearing up for the job. Don't let too much time pass from this point on. Look for the first opportunity to do the deed. If you have a job outside the home, spray the oven and let it sit while you are away. If you stay at home all day, let it sit overnight. Don't plan to use the oven for the next meal because you probably won't have time to finish the oven before the next meal.

Now that the oven is sprayed, you have to finish it up. But by now your mind has adjusted to it. Besides, now the oven can't be used until it is finished so there is no turning back. So jump in there, wipe up all the goo, *put down aluminum foil*, and you're done!

I don't think oven manufacturers like the aluminum foil idea because it somehow disperses the heat differently. I have used it for years and years, taking care that it doesn't touch the electric coils, and I love the fact that it catches the spillovers in the oven. But then I am not really a very good cook. Maybe using the foil has been my problem.

In two isolated cases, people have told me they have no trouble keeping their ovens clean. When I asked, in surprise, why not, both told me they use lots of aluminum foil—to line the oven and to enclose food when it's cooking so it won't spatter onto the sides and bottom of the oven. But then, maybe they aren't good cooks either.

This is a troublesome and weighty issue.

Three Easy Steps to a Cleaner Kitchen

1. Outlaw snacking unless you're present. Then be absent from the kitchen as often as possible.
2. Feed all animals in the garage. Unfortunately, children don't classify as animals, for this purpose.
3. Eat out.

PART 4

Helping the System Help You

19

On Procrastination

*An ounce of morning is worth
a pound of afternoon.*

What is that mysterious thing called *procrastination*? Why this chronic putting off of doing things when we know for sure that it is going to cause trouble later on? Why do we drop packages on the nearest chair instead of putting them away where they belong, put off paying the bills till they're late, toss clippings and mail in a pile, and leave the ice tray empty?

Like all things that have to do with human behavior, there probably are several reasons for this weakness, which apply in some combination to each of us.

Probably the main reason we put off doing things is because we are not organized to do a job. Either we don't have a place set up for what needs doing, or we don't have a plan for handling it.

Akin to this problem is having a place or plan that is so hard to use that we just don't get to it. If our file is out in the garage we aren't going to use it; we're going to put our papers in a pile until we go out. That setup is asking for trouble. If we don't have enough coat hangers or if the clothes rod is jammed so close to the shelf above it that it is hard to get the coat hangers in, we have a ready-made setup for procrastination.

We may put off writing checks to pay our bills because we really don't know how much money is in the bank. These are all organizational problems.

The more out of control a house becomes, the more there is to do, and the more impotent we become. On more than one occasion when my house has been in a total shambles, I have walked past a basket of clothes that needed folding and said to myself, I really must get to that, and then walked on.

The same is true of many other jobs, such as picking up a rubber band off the floor or filling the ice trays. I was forever passing things by. My housekeeping fuse was blown. Just as an electric circuit carries more and more electricity until it finally overloads and shuts down completely, so we keep going with more and more to do until our minds finally shut out what there is to do. It is almost impossible to get going again.

Thus procrastination is no mystery. It would be a miracle if a person did *not* put off doing things under these circumstances. Make it easy to do a job and you'll be much more likely to do it quickly.

Sometimes we procrastinate because we have let the job get so big that it has become very, very hard to do. One of the reasons Cleanies don't procrastinate is because they hate to do big jobs. They don't let big jobs develop because they know they won't want to do them and might procrastinate.

> The bitterness of living in a mess remains long after the sweetness of resting is forgotten.

I find that sometimes I put off doing something because I want the immediate gratification of some need. After a shopping trip, I am tired. I want to rest as soon as I get home. So I want to drop my packages, kick off my shoes, and lie down. I have reached the point now where the need to have an orderly, supportive home is more important than rest, so I am more likely to put away the things I bring in before I rest than to lie down and put them away later.

One of the most peculiar reasons for procrastination was one I noticed in myself after the change in my way of thinking took place. Somehow I had a vague feeling that someone else would do the job. Who, I do not know, but I definitely felt housework was not my job. Did I think I was an undiscovered princess, and the servants would do it? My favorite fairy tale was the one about the shoemaker who would awaken each morning to find that little elves had done all of his work during the night while he slept. Did I think little elves were frantically searching for my house and any day now, they would find it and surprise me? I don't know why I felt this way, but it certainly made me procrastinate.

There are other reasons for procrastination, such as lack of the clear-cut goal of having an orderly house. If this goal is lacking, it doesn't matter much whether a thing is done or not. Having such a pressured time schedule that we don't have time to do all that needs doing also encourages us to put off the harder jobs.

Recent research suggests a more mundane reason for procrastination that we would have noticed early on if we had just let ourselves: We have an aversion to doing some jobs. Rather than keeping a stiff upper lip, putting our noses to the grindstone, placing our shoulders to the wheel, and doing all of those other strange body activities people suggest, we don't do the job because we just don't like it. Knowing this enables us to face our own choices with clarity. Perhaps our choice is that we will do it even though we really would rather not. I think that is a part of maturity.

But there are other factors that influence our tendency to avoid the matter at hand. More appealing things call to us and give us an excuse not to do the unpleasant.

Reading. For bookworms, reading is quite a temptation—a wonderful way of escape into another world, which enables us to blot out the responsibilities around us. The piles around us grow dim as we lower our eyes to the book.

Daydreaming. Daydreaming, like reading, is a form of escape that takes time without showing results in the house. Sometimes we can use daydreaming about our house as an opportunity to set goals for it, but if we use up too much time daydreaming, what we daydream about never gets done.

Television. The television is one of the few modern electronics that has made a significant difference in our time use. The time it saps from other activities causes us to feel rushed when we get up from the TV.

How easy it is to flip a switch and step into another world. Once I got hooked on a soap opera, which became a problem because I felt I had to sit at home at a certain time for "my program." Housework faltered. Messies are particularly tempted by the TV syndrome because it gives a certain order to the day. The coming and going of the programs helps us to pace our time. In addition, if we plan to watch a program and then work, we feel we have accomplished one goal no matter how small.

Computer. Undoubtedly the computer vies with the television for free time in many households. Computer games, the internet, and email can be addictive. Hours fly by unnoticed and the house is forgotten.

Maybe it is not us who are hooked on the computer, but our family members, who should be joining us in keeping things up and are instead lost in cyberspace.

Visiting. The desire to talk to friends is strong. We tell ourselves that friends are more important than the house. Hours of escape time can be spent on the phone, at a friend's house over coffee, and so on—and our time for doing the housework is gone even when we vowed we were going to "get to it" that very day.

Turning the phone off, leaving it off the hook, screening calls with an answering machine, or just not answering unless it is a special ring from someone you have a prearrangement with are ways of cutting out this unplanned use of time. However it is done, cut down on talking time if it is a problem for you.

Leaving home. One definite way of escaping housework is to be absent from home. Too many social engagements, clubs, volunteer obligations, or shopping trips can effectively cut out the housekeeping chores. "I'm just so busy, I don't have time for housework." Sometimes extra reasons for leaving home such as making daily trips to the grocery store and ferrying children to too many functions eat up large blocks of time. Each one seems very reasonable in itself, until you add up the wasted time that you could have used more productively.

Perfectionism and high ideals. Spending the whole morning cleaning the oven or ironing wash-and-wear clothes, overdedication to playing with the children, or being meticulous about some other small aspect of the house or your personal life to the exclusion of the truly important jobs that need to get done are other ways of procrastinating. We're often trying to avoid the big jobs.

Sentimentality and regard for the old-fashioned ways. Baking your own cakes or bread, buying 100 percent cotton that needs ironing, doing windows the hard way, avoiding shortcut products, mixing your own cleaning products, or collecting trinkets for display that need dusting are time-consuming jobs that are so unrewarding we avoid doing them. Do you have some dusty pieces of clothing stored somewhere right now in a basket waiting for you to find time to iron them?

These are ways to escape from the important jobs we don't want to do. We do the easier jobs or more familiar jobs or the ones that we have to react to immediately because we have allowed an emergency to arise rather than setting goals and working toward those.

Stop and evaluate your use of time. Make a record for three days showing how your time is used. How much time do you actually allow for planned household tasks? You might be surprised that the statement "I don't have time for housework" is absolutely true because you make it that way.

How to Make Decisions

Another reason people procrastinate is that they hate to make decisions. Mary Beth was like that. Even deciding what to order at a restaurant with a big menu caused her a lot of confusion. Deciding where to store things in the house or when to do a job overwhelmed her.

Mary Beth's problem is a common one. She had grown to feel that her decisions were not always the best ones. Mother would criticize or suggest changes to improve Mary Beth's work. She always urged her to do better. Consequently, Mary Beth learned not to trust her own judgment. It was less painful not to decide than to run the risk of making the wrong decision. As a result, she became a procrastinator. It was so hard to decide how to organize her closet that she just left it alone. Leaving it alone, of course, was a decision—a decision not to tackle the job.

This hesitancy to make a decision and to start a job is due to anxiety and a poor self-image. On the other hand, making a decision can be an opportunity to feel in control, to assert one's desires, and to enhance one's self-image. It is a way for us to control, rather than to be controlled by, life.

What is the solution, then, to the inability to make decisions? How do you resolve the problem of procrastination? Several suggestions may help:

1. *Narrow your choices.* Give yourself permission not to try to do everything at once. Let's go back to Mary Beth's problem of deciding what to order at a restaurant. "I used to have that problem," her friend Esther said, "so I decided ahead of time on a pattern. When I eat out, I choose pork, beef, fish, and chicken, in that order. If I had fish last time I ate out, I know this time I'll choose chicken. It narrows my choices and makes my decisions easier."

2. *Predetermine many things.* The strength of the Flipper is this principle of deciding ahead on household chores.

3. *Set goals.* All decisions we make will move us in some direction. We need to determine ahead of time where we want to go. Then our decisions will be based on what we want to accomplish.

4. *Start!* The hardest part is starting because there are so many unknown decisions to be made, especially in a new activity. The reason that beginning is so important is because it is as we begin that we see what information

we will need. We can also see how the job is going to be organized. Remember, "A job begun is half done."

5. *Ask yourself, What is the worst that could happen?* Suppose you are afraid that the decision you make will not be the best. Ask, What is the worst that can come of this? Frequently the answer will surprise you. The big bad decision isn't as big as you thought when looked at in this light.

6. *Be willing to make a mistake.* You are not perfect, and you will make mistakes. It is a part of life.

7. *Get information.* Lack of information makes decisions harder than they need to be.

8. *Clear the base.* When the house, checkbook, laundry, and life in general are confused, it is no wonder that we have trouble deciding about anything. When our house and our schedule come under control, we have a better view of what we need and how to get it.

9. *Take control.* The turning point in decision making will come when we adopt the attitude that a decision to be made is an opportunity—not a threat.

Once we start to make decisions, we will have greater control over our tendency to procrastinate. Procrastination is not some vague weakness in our personality; there are definite causes for it. Find the demon in your life that causes you to procrastinate, and you will find that procrastination becomes a problem of the past.

In-Your-Face To-Do List

A lot of procrastination is just plain forgetfulness. So we need a workable to-do list.

Our list must be easily seen in order to be useful. With those of us who are Messies, bigger is almost always better. If my to-do list items are large enough and within my sight, I will remember to look at and do the items on the list. For that reason, my to-do list is a sheet of paper, about the size of poster board, which I place outside my office on the wall of the hall. Each time I pass I see my to-do list in big letters. It works. Slowly but surely, I cross off the items. Trust me, it works a lot better for me than any namby-pamby piece of paper. A large poster board or whiteboard with erasable markers will do just as well if you have a place you can easily display it.

Some people may find it useful to mark the to-do list off into four quadrants: Call, Do, Buy, Write. Having your activities designated into these four categories makes it a lot easier to see what you need to do.

Thirty-Second Rule

The thirty-second rule is this: If a task requires thirty seconds or less, do it right away. If we could build this rule into our lives, we would be much farther down the road to keeping our houses organized.

Thirty seconds is the time it takes to sing "Happy Birthday" very slowly. This presents a problem if you're singing it to time your activity. "Happy Birthday" drags even when it is sung at the normal speed. When sung slowly, it sounds like a funeral dirge. To solve that problem, I sing it twice in a very spritely tempo. It works out just the same.

Procrastinator's Creed

Knowing that procrastination is, at least in part, a matter of habit,
I will do the following as a matter of breaking the procrastination
habit:

I will make the bed as soon as it is empty.

I will fill the ice tray immediately and put it away.

I will put the toilet paper on the roll before it is half used.

I will clear the table, do the dishes, and clean the kitchen immediately after eating. I will consider cleanup a part of the meal.

I will put away what I get out and will not say I will be using it again soon.

I will put away my painting, ceramics, sewing, and other crafts when I am finished for the day, even if I will be using them tomorrow.

I will handle the mail as soon as I pick it up and will not leave it in a pile to consider later.

I will hang up my clothes and put away my shoes as soon as they are off my body.

I will be visually sensitive to anything out of place.

I will remember those three tender little words:

DO IT NOW!

which my conscience whispers when I am tempted to procrastinate.

20

On Making and Saving Time

What can be done at any time,
is never done at all.

ENGLISH PROVERB

Frequently we say we do not have enough time to keep house. This may be true in some cases. There are people who have so overscheduled their lives that they really don't have enough time at home to keep the house the way they would like to.

Aileen is one person who comes close to that state. She has a husband and handicapped son in the house. She works six days a week and on one of her free days a month goes to the garden club.

That leaves only three days a month free. Such a schedule makes housekeeping very difficult. Yet despite that, Aileen is making real progress because she is following the principles of good time management. Some women seem to be able to handle a schedule that is larger than life, but for most of us Messies it is wiser to schedule enough time to do what needs doing without Herculean effort. We are not, after all, superwomen.

Changes in Modern Time Use

You may be surprised to learn that a longitudinal thirty-year study by Robinson and Godbey reported in their book *Time for Life* shows that American adults today have five hours more free time a day than in 1965. Our total amount of free time is about forty hours a week. There is no significant difference in free time between men and women. By free time we mean discretionary time not given over to employment, housework, self-care, sleeping, or any of the activities necessary for living. Free time includes television viewing, reading, hobbies, recreation, socializing, religious and cultural events, and adult education. For us it could include getting the house under control.

Hard as it is to believe, compared to 1965,

- Americans are not working longer hours on their jobs.
- Women's total work time is not significantly higher than men's.
- Parents are not spending less time with their children.
- Americans are not spending less time on sleep, meals, or religion.

The experience of many people makes this very hard to believe. In addition to our own experiences of feeling very strapped for time, expert testimony tells us through the media that we are becoming more and more rushed and our free time is diminishing. But the hard facts do not bear this out.

Part of this is because less housework is being done both by women in the paid workforce and by full-time homemakers. Men are doing 33 percent of the housework, according to data from 1985, while they were doing only 15 percent of the housework in 1965. Another interesting fact in the area of housekeeping is that although employed women spend 40 percent less time doing housework than full-time homemakers, their homes were not rated significantly less tidy by interviewers or the women themselves.

Now there's a thought-provoking bit of information! It bears out the validity of the suggestions given in the rest of this chapter. It is not so much how much time you have as how you use it.

Use Little Minutes

When we say we don't have enough time, usually we have an organizational problem. We do have a few minutes here and there, but because we are not prepared with plans or don't remember what those plans are because they are not on our to-do list, the time slips by without our noticing. There are a lot of "little minutes" to be found between large blocks of time if we are just prepared to use them.

It is strange to think that the simple management of minutes can make such a difference in our lives. Actually it is at this point that Cleanies differ markedly from Messies. Cleanies value little minutes. They use little bits and pieces of time whenever they have them and consequently get a lot done without ever seeming to have to do long hours of housework. They do such things as clean the tub as soon as they get out, wipe the sink after they brush their teeth, and hang up clothes as soon as they take them off.

The use of these little minutes will make the difference between success and failure.

A peculiarity of mine, and perhaps of yours, is the habit of thinking only of big jobs. If there is a little piece of paper on the floor, I sigh to myself, *I guess I'll have to vacuum the floor*, and walk on by. My Cleanie friends would stoop down, pick up the paper, and finish the job.

I think this idea of the *big job* is a peculiar attempt at organizing on our parts. We react to the idea of doing a job rather than just doing the part that is a problem.

The reason for this no doubt is because we are "thought people," not "visual people." We would rather plan an activity in an orderly fashion and then do it (or maybe never do it; but at least it is neatly planned) than do a little bit at a time. Perhaps this is an attempt to stop the flitting around and distractibility that afflicts the Messie. But, like other good ideas that don't work, it needs to be abandoned.

Make the Bed

Never before has bed making been so easy. The popularity of fluffy comforters means that we don't have to straighten the sheets underneath as neatly as we used to. You can hide your cat under there and nobody would know. Because the comforter turns down at the top, we don't have to cover the pillows just so with the spread. Because of pillow shams, we can position the pillows we use to sleep on at the top of the bed and throw the shamcovered pillows over them.

You should be able to make the bed with only one visit to each side. Two minutes tops.

The area of the bed covers a large percentage of the bedroom. It is the largest piece of furniture in the house. If it is neat, it sets an orderly tone for the rest of the house.

The fact that you make it as soon as you get up sets a tone for the day as well. You are saying to yourself and the house that you have a "can-do" attitude.

Warning: Don't use all of those little decorative pillows so fashionable nowadays. They are a nuisance to take off and put on.

Don't make the sheets that are covered by the comforter too neat. As a matter of fact, you might want to leave wrinkles deliberately just to get out of the perfectionistic habit of aiming for wrinkle-free sheets. This is not the army. You have better things to do.

Cooking Time

Some jobs require a certain amount of thought and planning. Meal preparation is one example.

Cooking and shopping for food take a great deal of time. To speed up that process, plan menus and shopping lists for a week or so in advance. Sample menus and a shopping guide for one week are given below. As mentioned earlier, several weeks done like this can be made a part of the Flipper.

Sample Weekly Menu

Sunday	baked soy chicken, rice, brussels sprouts, rolls
Monday	hot dogs, sauerkraut, macaroni and cheese, sliced tomatoes
Tuesday	spaghetti with meat sauce, mixed green salad, Italian bread
Wednesday	fish sticks, baked potato halves, peas, slaw
Thursday	cheese omelet, sausage, broccoli, biscuits
Friday	tuna-noodle casserole, green beans, applesauce
Saturday	broiled fish fillets, parsley rice, glazed carrots, rolls

Also look for easy but good recipes. Cookbooks and magazines offer lots of "fast and easy" recipes. Occasionally bringing in take-out food will take off the pressure during a busy day. Eating out and take-home food are extremely popular in some areas of the country. If not overdone, these certainly can be a help from time to time.

Double cooking is always a good idea. Make twice as much spaghetti sauce or bake two chickens so that another meal is basically started.

One of the ideas I like best is for the husband to take his turn at cooking. In my family, my husband is the head barbecuer. In Florida, where we have so much warm weather, we can do a lot of barbecuing.

Question: What does the busy wife make for supper?
Answer: Reservations!

Don't let the family fall into the habit of eating at different times. This will wreck time schedules and is not ideal for family life.

Shopping

Write grocery lists according to your grocery store layout and save yourself lots of dead time going from aisle to aisle. But our shopping needs are not limited to food. Consider how much time you spend shopping for nonfood and even for nonclothing items.

According to Juliet Schor in *The Overworked American*, Americans spend three to four times as many hours a year shopping as their European counterparts. In addition to using time in shopping, the goods we buy require time to maintain, store, and use. The average American consumes twice as much as he or she did forty years ago. Buy less to save time both in shopping and maintenance.

Catalogs save shopping time and energy. I like catalog shopping because of its convenience and because there are things offered in catalogs that aren't carried in the stores. You go from one department to another with the flip of a page. Ordering sizes has problems, but these usually can be worked out. Hard-to-get sizes are carried in catalogs, too.

Gift house catalogs carry many items I have found useful for organizing my house. Frequently the items, like storage shelves of certain types, are not easy to find in the store but are staples of this kind of catalog.

Whatever you are shopping for in a store, don't waste time while you do it. If possible, shop when the crowds are down. A full-time homemaker said to me, "It is a sin for me to grocery shop on a Saturday or a Friday night." If you can, avoid shopping at those times.

Shopping on the internet is perhaps the easiest of all—so easy we have to make sure we set boundaries on our spending.

Time Stretchers

Everybody has twenty-four hours a day, but some people seem to manage those hours better than other people do. Consider how the following time stretchers could add minutes or even hours to your day:

Double Up Entertaining

Once the house is company ready, invite guests on back-to-back days. Or have twice as many people over as you usually would; this makes *one* evening, *one* cooking, and *one* cleanup. Or have an open house for a very large number; then you kill lots of birds with one stone, saving gobs of time.

Know Where Things Are

How much time is wasted looking? Have a hook for keys just inside the door; have an eyeglasses holder; have a file for bills.

Plan for Easy Maintenance

Don't buy white rugs, clothes that need ironing, longhaired dogs, or knickknacks that need dusting. When you buy something, ask yourself, *Will it cause me work to maintain it?* Usually, because we are in love with the idea of how nice it will be to have an item and because we don't regard maintenance as very important, we buy what we like no matter how poor a choice it is from the maintenance standpoint.

Don't Do So Much

If you sat down and listed all your activities, you would probably be shocked at all that has crawled into your life while you weren't looking. Look at your schedule with clear eyes. Then begin weeding out. Vegetables that are planted too close together jam each other so tightly that none develop properly. In order to have full, healthy vegetables, some good plants have got to go to leave room for the others. Some of us have so much jammed together that none of our activities are really producing well. The quality of life improves as the quantity of activities is reduced, if we have overscheduled ourselves.

Once you decide what you want to keep in your life, list all of your projects and the first step to take in accomplishing each task. Trying to remember everything you have on the burners of your mind will wear you out. When you have a few moments to spare, you won't remember what activity you can fit in unless it is on your project list.

Store Things Where They Will Be Used

Apply all of the storage ideas we have mentioned. Store cleaning materials in each bathroom. Store towels in the bathroom, if possible. Keep the dishes by the dishwasher and the pots and pans by the stove. And know where they are stored. Use labels. Nothing wastes time in a more frustrating way than looking for a lost or misplaced item.

Manage Telephone and Visiting Time

If a lot of time is wasted talking, either in person or on the telephone, set your own time limits. If you plan to work on the house until 10 a.m., don't accept calls before then. If 6 p.m. to 8 p.m. is your time for the children, explain to the callers that you are busy and will call them back. Or screen calls with your answering machine, voice mail, and caller ID.

Initially, the answering machine was used to catch the calls that came in while the owner was away. It became quickly obvious that the answering machine could also protect the time of the person who is at home by screening the calls.

The plans and schedules of distractible folks can be seriously interfered with by interrupting telephone calls. Screening can solve that problem. After your message is played, if you are home you can hear the message as it is being given by the caller. If you wish to pick up you can. The best idea is probably to return all calls at one time. Since you are the person who initiated the call when you return it, you have more initiative when it comes to saying good-bye. So by screening your calls, you have more control over when you talk and how long you talk.

Sometimes when I pick up to answer while a message is being left, the caller will ask, "Are you screening your calls?" I don't know what their point is in asking, but I always answer enthusiastically and cheerfully, "Absolutely! What can I do for you?"

When I am screening my calls but keeping an ear out for those calls that I want to answer, I set the volume of the machine up so I can hear it in several surrounding rooms. To make things even easier, I keep the cordless phone with me wherever I am so that I can pick up quickly when I hear who it is.

The final advantage of the answering machine is that many nuisance calls hang up when they hear an answering machine. That's a real time-saver.

Lenore uses a head phone set with her cordless phone so she can exercise by walking or can dust and straighten while she talks.

Move Fast

In my interviews with Cleanies, I was surprised at the recurring comment, "I move fast" or, "I don't waste time getting it done." Cleanies want to get their housekeeping goals accomplished and move on to other things. As a Messie, I must admit that I took a more casual approach. One reason Cleanies move fast is that they have a definite time goal for the completion of their schedules.

Ask for Help

In Proverbs 31, the chapter about the ideal woman, you will notice tucked away in verse 15 a mention of her maidens. This woman had help with all her enterprises! We need outside help, too. We need a certain number of electronic maidens to help us with our work. Electronic dishwashers, washing machines, dryers, microwave ovens—all can be useful in our busy days.

Time research indicates that none of these gadgets actually saves time. They just allow us to do more. When automatic washing machines became a part of life, families just washed more clothes. Microwaves enable us to cook our meals faster but do not cut down on the real time-consuming part of cooking, food preparation.

There is a point at which too many gadgets become counterproductive, and we have to spend more time cleaning appliances and more space storing them than they are worth. Don't overdo in this area.

Buy Time

If you have more jobs than time to do them in, buy somebody else's time.

Just because your friends do okay without help or because somebody else in your family did what you are trying to do without hiring help does not mean that you need to deny yourself what you need. No two situations are the same.

I spoke with a mother of six young children who could easily afford to hire outside help but decided to tough it out alone as a matter of principle. And she was really struggling. If you can, get outside help to supplement your efforts. Don't feel guilty about it, either. You are not neglecting your responsibilities; you are just buying more time when you need it.

Unfortunately, a cleaner is not the answer to the basic problem. One woman said she had a full-time maid but still had a problem. The maid just kept her piles dusted. Another said her cleaning person charged her ten dollars more to clean than she charged a neighbor, because the work at her house was so much harder. Basically, you are the only one who can organize for yourself.

Then there is the problem of cleaning up for the cleaner. We would be embarrassed to have anyone come in and see the place in its usual condition. Some houses aren't ready yet.

Sometimes you can hire someone to come and help with your organizational project as well as your cleaning if she is someone you feel you can work with in this way. Professional organizers are an option.

After you have developed your organizational system and have listed the chores for each day, you can give whoever helps you the jobs of your heavy day and be free to do what you like. She is best used for maintenance. This is when she can be of real help to you.

It is tempting to try to use her to do what no one person can do—keep the house all week with just a one-day visit. You must follow your own daily plan of maintenance and break old habits if your house is going to look nice for more than one day a week.

If you decide to get outside help, the most satisfactory way to find someone is through the recommendation of a friend. If you don't know anyone who can help you with a recommendation, ask around to find out how people in your area have found help.

21

Getting the Family to Cooperate

*It is easier to rule a kingdom
than to regulate a family.*

JAPANESE PROVERB

If there is one place where your program will run into trouble, it will be with getting your family to cooperate. Read the following letter:

Dear Messies Anonymous,

The house is a mess now, and I don't feel very good about myself for it. I look out the window quite often to make sure no company is coming. One time I was in the mood for cleaning and my children said, "Who is coming?" Now that's bad! I have three children, ages fifteen, eight, and eighteen months. Since the baby was born, it really got worse. I wish I was very neat, but I am not.

Is it normal at all to have a messy house? I see some mess in my house and it depresses me. I am ashamed. I know I need help. My fifteen-year-old daughter helps when asked but even that doesn't help in the big mess. My eight-year-old son does not help, even when asked, nor does my husband. I should not have to ask. I should be able to do it all. But I don't. I know I will never win the "Tammy Tidy" award, but there must be a better way.

Please help, M.F.

This lady's problem is typical. Let's be realistic. Just because you have a desire to live a different life doesn't mean the rest of the family is going to have the same desire at exactly the same time as you do. And you must realize that you may be largely responsible for the bad habits that have developed, especially in the children. Habits are not broken in a day, or in a week. It takes patience and determination within ourselves to overcome these obstacles. A big dose of humor and love toward our family is important.

But we should also develop a plan of approach. First, you will need to communicate your dream. Have a family meeting about three weeks after you begin your new program. You will have established your credibility by this time. Write out a goal-setting daydream to read to them.

You may also want to share the following letter with your family:

To the family of a Reforming Messie:

Someone close to you wants very much to change her way of life so that the house is not a problem.

The decision to change is a significant one and she will need your help in that decision. Keeping house is a very complex job. The Reforming Messie is one who has become bogged down in that complexity but is not willing to live that way anymore. She feels a change is necessary; no, *imperative!*

The house is our home base. It is the extension of ourselves into our surroundings. When visitors come unexpectedly and we are embarrassed, when we cannot invite friends over because it is too much work to prepare, when we can't find the important papers (birth certificate, insurance bill, income tax information, and so on), our way of life suffers and so does our self-concept.

And then there is the confusion. Why does so-and-so have such a neat and lovely home while I struggle and fail? Is there something wrong with me? If so, what is it?

On the other hand, when the house becomes neat, orderly, and beautiful not only on the surface but on the inside as well, a sense of control, confidence, and worth comes to replace frustration and guilt.

As the Messie begins to put this program into practice, you may notice some peculiar differences. There may be several responses from you to this change.

If you tend to be what we call a Cleanie (one for whom keeping the house neat comes easily), you may applaud what you see. All the confusion and clutter has been driving you crazy. At last you see a ray of hope. Let me encourage you to do what you can to help, but be patient and understanding. Now is not the time to take over and give all those hints and suggestions you always wanted to give. Don't rush things. The change must come from within, even if it comes more slowly than you would like. There may be slips backward that will discourage both you and your Messie. But remember, a detour is not a dead end. With encouragement things will get on course again.

If you yourself have the tendency to be a Messie, you may have difficulty adjusting to this new way of life. You may be a Messie who is frustrated with this problem of messiness. You, like the Messie you live with, have been upset by this lack of control and the problems it brings to your life. Maybe you feel ready to tackle changing and join in the changing. For you the adjustment will be easy. You will be relieved. Or you may want things neater and more organized but may not be willing as yet to make any changes yourself to bring order. Or you may be one who says, "It doesn't matter to me what the house is like. I wish she would just leave things alone." What you need to realize is that having a nice house is very important to someone close to you and you have an important part in it.

When a person decides to change housekeeping habits, it involves the family in a way other changes do not. If a person decides to stop overeating, drinking, or smoking, it is pretty much an individual endeavor requiring only encouragement and patience from the family. In the area of housekeeping, the family is much more involved in the change because the family functions in that house each day. The once easygoing Messie now becomes concerned if you get out the telephone book and don't put it away when you are through. Your shoes in the living room, once ignored, now become a problem. You may wonder if things weren't better before all this "wonderful" change started. Many times you will be *positive* things were better before all this neatness craze began.

Your understanding at this point is crucial. What the Reforming Messie is undergoing is a new experience. For the first time, the house is a priority and for the first time she feels that there is hope. For the first time she is struggling with control in an area she has been defeated in before. When new things are attempted, it takes practice—for her to know how to approach you about the change and for you to know how to respond. So be understanding, be patient, and above all, be cooperative.

Change is always hard, but it is worth it, not just to the Reforming Messie but also to you. You will probably find after a time that you are changed and wouldn't want another way of life for the world either.

Training Your Children

Communicating your dream will not be enough. "Many hands make light work." Translated into home life, this means that every member of the family must help with the solution since every member is part of the problem. Part of the reason that my friend Marcella's house is always nice is that her six-year-old has been well trained and always puts her things away.

One way to do this is to put in writing every task that you want your family to help with. Then it is not your *saying* the job must be done; it is the written instruction that requires the job to be done. Writing, especially typing, is much more official than Mom. Mom's voice fades quickly and can be forgotten. Writing stays there until it is dealt with.

The Flipper will set up your household tasks in writing with a job for every member of the family. Say, "Jack, do your job before dinner." Remember, this is a nice way of saying, "You can't eat until you do the job." This food idea can carry over to cleaning his room as well. It seems to be standard procedure for organized mothers who have their families under control.

Don't forget to let him mark it off or see you mark it off, and don't forget to say thanks as you do so. I have found people are amazingly cooperative when you are working with a checklist and not just telling them what to do.

In addition to communicating what you want, you must let kids know you are serious about what you have them do by checking it after it is done. I repeat, people do what you *in*spect, not what you *ex*pect. Don't assume or hope that what you tell them to do will get done; inspect it and give praise or a reward for a job well and quickly done.

This is where many of us fail with our children. It is so much easier to assume they have done what they should without actually checking. And being easily distracted, as many of us are, it is hard to remember to check each time. But kids need to know that the job will be checked each time.

Finally, don't let the kids make a big mess. Kids can make a bigger mess than they can clean up. One reason we have a hard time getting them to clean up their toys—the tent made of sheets, the tea set out with all the dolls sitting around it, the pillows propped around for furniture, and the cookies, and the thermos with juice in it—is simply because it is too much for them to handle. It doesn't make sense to allow them to bring it all out and not make them put it back, does it? "You kids brought all this junk out and now you are going to put it right back where you got it. I want all that stuff put away before your father gets home. Now let's get busy!"

It is much easier for children to get things out of their proper places, to unfold the sheet and so on, than it is to fold the sheet and collect and wash the pieces of the tea set. Besides, now they are tired and their attention span is spent.

What is the answer? Frankly, I love to make a big mess. There is a certain wonderful freedom in living without restraint if only for an afternoon. I don't do it anymore, however, because really I don't want the problem of cleaning up a colossal mess or living with it if I don't clean it up. The "freedom" is not worth it to me. But because I know the joy of making a big mess, I tend to let the kids do the same thing, thinking I am doing them a favor. Then they are left with the problem I have learned to avoid in my own life. That's really not fair to them.

So the answer is to help the kids plan. You put some limitations on how much they can get out, where they can put it, how long they can play. They will want more things and time than you will allow, but soon they will get used to living less excessively and you will get used to directing them in a more moderate way. At first you will have more work to do because you won't be able to leave them on their own. I have noticed that children of Cleanies play more neatly than mine

212

because the limitations on their activities were started earlier in childhood.

Be sure to tell your children ahead of time how long they can play. Then tell them ten minutes before the time elapses that they will have to quit and clean up in ten minutes and stick by that time schedule.

Behavior modification is another method to change sloppy habits of children. This requires serious thought to set up a plan for your needs. First decide what one specific habit you want to work on changing. Is it leaving toys in the living room, dropping books by the door, not making the bed, not hanging up the clothes? Work on that one thing and offer a reward for improvement. If there is more than one child, have them work together as a team. If the team succeeds in breaking the habit for that day, they are rewarded immediately. If one falls down, the team has to wait until the next day for the opportunity to achieve a reward. Be careful to encourage an upbeat atmosphere. Don't criticize the one who fails. Cheer success.

Remember you don't want to cause a mess in your family life while trying to straighten out the house. The house is for the family, so care is required to maintain love and good humor while making the change.

As in all things, love and patience go a long way in making the transition. It also helps to have some nice activity planned for them when they have finished with the cleanup.

Kids and Their Rooms

The *Kansas City Star* ran a messy room contest and found that "many mothers attached notes with their entries, begging for advice on that age-old problem: how to motivate their children to 'clean up that room!'" When the newspaper contacted Joanie

Nicholas, a local professional organizer, about the problem, her reply was, "Kids need to see an example of their parents putting things away. They need to clean up together, maybe every Saturday."

She continued by saying that if a parent simply orders a youngster to clean his bedroom, "at best the child will just shove everything under the bed and into the closet."

The second-place winner was a girl of eleven. Her picture showed a room strewn with clothes a foot deep including a muddy rubber boot, empty containers and lids, and stuffed toys. She insisted that her room looked like this on purpose: "It's just, like, cool that way, because everything's spread out and you know where everything is."

Some parents firmly expect children to keep their rooms presentable (not perfect) and also help with the house. Others seem helpless because the children add to the mess. The first group of parents are the happy ones with neat houses. Attitude is everything. How do they do it? How can you do it?

Think of Your Children's Future as Adults

You want them to be prepared for the real world, when no one else will pick up after them. These are habits that last a lifetime. If you raise tidy children, someday their spouses will love you for it.

Teach by Showing

When teaching skills such as bed making and table setting, work side by side with children for as long as it takes to make sure they know how to do a job. Then stay with them the next few times until you are sure they can do it on their own. Praise them for their efforts. Make paper placemats with drawings of silverware to aid young children in placement when setting the table.

Make It a Team Effort

Put two or three jobs a day on the list for each person in the house, including adults. Little people get simpler jobs. Check them off as done. The fact that parents have jobs on the list and are checking themselves off will inspire the children to do their jobs.

Organize Schedules

Keep a large yearly calendar in view. Write each scheduled activity on the calendar without fail. Next to the calendar, place a desktop filing system with a hanging file folder for every family member. Put school information, invitations, etc. in the appropriate folder for easy access.

Make It Easy for the Kids

Simplify everyone's life with these tips.

1. Every child needs a filing cabinet for his or her school and personal papers. Include a separate hanging file for each year's treasures.
2. Too many toys? Divide them into three or four boxes. Rotate the boxes on a weekly basis. This cuts down on shelf storage space.
3. Bag sets of things with their instructions. Allow only one bag out at a time. Mark the backs of puzzle pieces so they can easily be replaced in the appropriate bag.
4. Little toys can be stored on the back of the door in shoe holders.

5. Lower the clothes hanging bar in the closet if the child can't reach it. Cut a PVC pipe to the proper length, run a rope through it, and tie the rope to the bar above at both ends. Place step stools where necessary.

6. Limit cleanup time. Play a song or set a timer and say, "Let's see how many toys we can pick up before the end."

7. Limit cleanup activities. Say, "I'll pick up six and you pick up six. Then we are through."

8. Use the "Happy Birthday Rule." If it only takes thirty seconds (stuff like putting away the book bag), the job should be done immediately.

9. Attach a checklist by the light switch for the child to check before leaving the room in the morning. The first thing on the list should be MAKE BED, because once the bed is made the room is 50 percent straight. For small children, post picture reminders.

Remember: Nothing works automatically. The success of these ideas is up to the parents. So keep your focus. For more information about a family team approach read my book *Neat Mom, Messie Kids*.

Training Your Husband

Husband training is another matter, and I could not presume to tell you how to work most effectively with your husband. Each marriage is different and each relationship is different. If you make housekeeping an issue between the two of you, you may lose more than you gain.

In my family I find the most effective method is to get the house in very good order; then things that are out of place stand out glaringly. Nobody likes to mess up an orderly area.

However, this is not always the whole answer. After twenty-three years of living with me, my husband had developed some poor habits too. It is hard to say what he would have been like had he married a Cleanie. One day when I had concluded he was not showing the proper concern for my goals in the house, I decided to do what I suggest my students do: "If you have a need, talk about it."

So I talked, not in a grudging way but in a way that expressed my feelings. To my amazement, my husband told me his view of how things were going and it made sense. I had not noticed some of the ways he had been contributing, and his heart was with me. Knowing this took a lot of pressure off my mind.

Sure, things go awry now and again. Sure, I have my weaknesses and he has his. But he lets me know about mine, I let him know about his, and we make adjustments and move on—usually in the right direction.

Perhaps you have tried talking but it made little difference. You might try writing how you feel to him:

Dear Hubby,

First let me say I love you. You have brought so many strengths to my life and to our marriage, and I really appreciate that.

I am bringing to you a problem I have. For a long time I have been struggling with myself and with the house, trying to get control over the clutter. And believe me, it is a struggle.

The only reason I keep trying is because it bothers me so much to live never knowing where things are or having to wade through so much stuff to look for something. It worries me that important papers may be lost in the piles. (I know they are probably there—but where?) I am afraid people may drop in unannounced. I want to be able to have guests over without having to go through Herculean efforts.

Most of all I guess I want to live in a beautiful house that I feel is under control. Perhaps you and I are different in how we feel, but I'll bet that if things were beautiful and under control, you would feel the same sense of joy I would and be proud of how the house looks. So I would like you to do two things: First, I hope you will share with me my goal for a new way of life. Only if we stand together in this will we even begin to make any progress.

Second, I want to ask you to help by putting away the things you get out like ice cream bowls, magazines, and shoes. Also I want you to help me clean up and get rid of the unnecessary things around the house.

It will be a big job and require a lot of effort from both of us, but let's do it together.

I can't wait until we have made the change.

Loving you,

Now you may expect any number of responses, from enthusiasm (not likely), to bafflement, to reluctance or maybe worse. Work with whatever attitude you get. If your husband's response is not satisfactory, have patience. Patience, I have found, is a big ingredient in marriage. Usually it pays off if it is born of love and commitment to each other.

Newton's law of inertia says that any body of matter at rest tends to stay that way unless some force moves it to get it started. Translated into housework, it means it won't be easy to break old patterns. Do as much changing as your husband will permit at a time, and you will probably find the going gets easier as you move along. It is not easy, but it is worthwhile.

Talking, setting up a system, writing—all of these are valuable. If they work, fine. If not, you need to think of communicating by actions. My book *When You Live with a Messie* deals with the problem by suggesting that a powerful way to influence behavior change is to stop protecting the messy person from the results of his messiness.

When leaving his underwear on the floor means he runs out of underwear, that gets his attention. If you pick up the underwear, put it in the hamper, wash it, and replace it in his drawer, you are not letting his problem impact his life. If you kick clothes he drops on the floor into the back of the closet after you have told him that you will wash only clothes put into the hamper, you help him to understand how his messy actions impact his life. Invite people over. If you cease having friends in, you protect him from the results of his messy behavior. Having friends over gives some Messies the urge to get their stuff up.

This is a complicated issue because it deals with important relationships we need to preserve while we are solving the organizing problems of the house. That's why I wrote a whole book about it.

How to Get Family Help around the House

- Hide the kitten, then ask your daughter if it could be trapped under the junk in her closet.
- Tell your teenage son it's time his new girlfriend was given an escorted tour of the house—including his room.
- Let your husband's socks lie where they fall until he panics at 6:00 one cold morning.
- Leave the dog's half-chewed bone where it is—between the bedroom and the back door—then wait until your husband has to let the dog out at 4 a.m.

22

More Tips on Organizing

*Doing housework the hard way is for
those who have nothing better to do.*

It is my goal for all of you, and for me too, that we should get
and keep our homes organized in the least possible amount
of time. A stay-at-home woman has better things to do than
spend more time than necessary organizing and cleaning. If
you work and don't spend all day at home, you will have less
time and less energy for housekeeping. Nevertheless, your goal
can be achieved!

Clear Surfaces

To accomplish this, a lot of cluttered surfaces need to be cleared.
Special temptations for clutter are the top of the toilet tank and
the bathroom window ledge. Kitchen windows, and kitchen
counters too, fairly beg to have things put on them: bottles,

jars, tissue boxes, and appliances. The clutter turns any dream of cleaning these surfaces into a nightmare. There is no such thing as a quick swipe at the bathroom or kitchen in your morning cleaning when all these things have to be moved.

The best way to achieve order in the bathroom is to get a shower caddy and put the shampoo and conditioner bottles, the soap, and the washcloths on it.

In the kitchen, I suggest an almost bare counter. For a long time I fought this idea. I noticed that two of my Cleanie friends had almost completely bare counters. Still, I resisted clearing my kitchen counter because I thought it was an unnecessary and rather extreme step.

Then, in reading a book on housecleaning, I again came upon the bare counter idea. That made it official! If it's in a book it carries more weight, so I tried it. What a difference it made!

Clearing my kitchen counter and color coding my clothes in the closet were the two moves that had the most satisfactory results for me. I didn't think either one was particularly important, but both turned out to be significant helps. I took the canisters off the counter and distributed them in several separate places in the kitchen cabinets. I put the blender under the counter in a place that had been cleared by throwing away some unused item. I felt I had to leave my toaster and my coffeemaker on the counter, although my Cleanie friends keep theirs underneath. But since then I have gotten rid of my toaster, so that spot on the counter is empty. When my family wants toast, I broil it in the oven.

Now you are going to tell me that you don't have room under your counter. I know the problem. I am sure that men design kitchens and have no idea how much room is necessary for storage.

However, let me tell you of one woman's experience. She had her kitchen remodeled. During the remodeling, she put her kitchen equipment on a table on the back porch. After the remodeling was finished, she decided to leave it on the porch and get items to be stored in the kitchen only as she needed them. At the end of three months, half the things were still on the back porch. If you used this method, how much would be superfluous and left on the back porch?

I know the potato ricer belonged to Grandmother and the pots were Uncle Henry's, but you have the here and now to think of. Can you think of a way to clear out the space under the counter so you can clean off the top?

Avoid Messes

Another way to cut down cleaning time by changing organizational patterns is to plan not to let things get dirty. An ounce of prevention is worth a pound of cleaning up. Thus, you can put rugs both inside and outside the entrance doors so that dirt and trash will get caught there before being dragged into the house. You can put foil on the bottom of the oven so that if anything spills, all you need to do is change the foil rather than clean the oven. You can use cook-in bags for things that might splatter. If you don't have a cook-in bag, at least use a pot with very high sides.

One of the hardest problems for me to deal with was soap scum in the bathroom from the hand soap. It melted into the soap dish and foamed over the side, hardening into a kind of cement. I hated it.

Luckily, just at the time I was ready to do something about it, soft soap became popular. That was my solution. The only problem was that it was quickly used up by my teenagers.

I decided to save soap slivers from bar soap and mush them into an empty liquid soap dispenser, adding perfume to the mixture to give it class. If we lived during war years when soap was rationed, this would make sense. But in today's world, it was crazy, left over from my inappropriately frugal days. Cheap liquid soap would do the trick just as well.

As for those slivers, now I throw them away even though I know that they have just a little use left to them. That is sanity.

Be Proactive

Another method to speed up cleaning is to spot chronic problem areas and look for a solution. I had a trash can for throwing away food in my kitchen. It had no top because I thought it would be too much of a problem to remove the top each time, and it would be too difficult to do with scraps in my hand. The can was not very satisfactory because it was unsightly and the food kept splattering onto the white wall behind it, requiring frequent wiping with bleach and soap.

When I finally awoke to the fact that this was a chronic problem that needed a solution, I was tuned in to solving it though I didn't have any idea how I would do it. I was just waking up to the simple facts of housekeeping life.

Soon afterward I was wandering through a discount store and saw a garbage can with a lid and a foot pedal that opened the lid. This kept the food scraps covered, and when the top lifted back it protected the white wall from streaks and spots of garbage entering the can. I had seen these cans frequently but, until I had identified my specific cleaning problem, I had not really considered getting one for my kitchen. If you identify a problem with a view to solving it, often the solution soon comes knocking at your door.

Keep on Top of Clutter

The final way to organize for order is to put things away. This is a very hard habit to get into, but it is a top priority.

I learned a little about this on the day after Thanksgiving. The shopping center was really crowded. The shoe store salesmen were bustling around. Shoe boxes and shoes were everywhere, some piled by the customer and some where the customer had been before.

There came a slight lull and the manager began clucking around the store, "Are these your shoes, Bill? Are these yours, Cal? Check these boxes—whose are they?"

When I asked him how he kept all these boxes and shoes straight, he gave me these tips:

1. Don't let too much time go by between straightening up. Keep things up.
2. Each salesman is responsible for an area of the store, so the manager has an idea who is falling down on the cleaning job when he sees what area is messy.
3. Every time a salesman goes in the back to get another shoe, he takes something with him whether it is his or not.
4. The fourth thing he did not tell me—I saw it. It was that he had his standard and he personally saw that the system worked.

The application to the home is obvious:

1. Keep short accounts—don't let things get too far behind.
2. Devise an easy-to-manage plan, so you can check on how each person is doing his or her job.

3. Everybody does his or her part and works as a team to get the job done.
4. Don't rely on the plan working by itself. We check on it and nudge it along.

These tips apply to all aspects of home management, even grocery shopping.

When you bring the groceries in, put them away, fold the bags, and either store them immediately or throw them out. No fair using the groceries out of the bag or, worse still, out of the car. You've got to put them away.

This principle applies to laundry, which should be folded and put away immediately. I've discovered that I can save energy by sorting the laundry while the piles are small and manageable. I also put the piles in the order of the ages of family members. Then I don't have to figure out where each pile is. That speeds things up a lot. Mail should be thrown away or filed immediately, too. When I write a letter, I put it in the mailbox immediately. So far it hasn't been stolen or rained on. Business executives, early in their careers, learn the value of handling papers only once. As executives of our own homes, we can apply this principle to our own work. Handle small chores as they come up; don't wait for them to add up to a mighty mountain of work.

But where and how do you get charged up for your work? Read on!

Deal with the Sentimental Past

Ah, the past. We can't live with it all around us in the form of mementos, trinkets, papers, and (let's face it) just pure junk, which is important to us because it proves we lived. Getting rid of these things feels like getting rid of a part of ourselves. Some ideas we can use are these:

Tastefully display the important mementos. If you have a long hall where you can display your family portraits or a display case for your valuable mementos, obviously these are the places for them. Go to it. Get those items on display now. Don't leave them in a pile and say, "I'll do it someday."

Use a memory journal. Write down the activities of the day, especially the nice ones. You don't have to include your personal or deep thoughts, though you can if you wish. By conserving your life in this way, you won't need to keep the useless receipts, wrappers, letters, etc. that you now use to document your existence. These pages will be invaluable not only to you but to your children, grandchildren, and great grandchildren.

Box up and store mementos. Token remembrances also can be kept, of course, in easy-to-store, labeled plastic shoe boxes. But remember, keep only token items—not everything.

Move the past out of your present life. If you can't seem to come to terms with getting rid of the past, at least clear it away. Do that by boxing it into those white twelve-by-fifteen-inch banker's boxes can buy at office supply stores. Document where you store them by using the card storage system in your box or listing the boxes and their contents on the computer. Store them in the garage, basement, attic, or (gasp) in a rented public storage unit.

Once you get them out of your way, you will be able to see how much better life is without all of this stuff around. I know that for many, these items are friends. At first it will be hard to live without having them in close proximity. But the freedom you will feel later is worth the initial discomfort.

Ten Commandments of Housekeeping

1. Thou shalt not try to do everything thyself. Get help from thy children, husband, and professional cleaners as you can.
2. Thou shalt have a goal, for without a goal, nothing will be accomplished.
3. Thou shalt have a plan and stick to it.
4. Remember the family, to treat them in love while you (and they) are changing.
5. Thou shalt not overschedule and thou shalt not say yes to everyone who asks. Set your own priorities and say yes or no in line with them. Take control of your activities.
6. Thou shalt dream and keep dreaming until your lifestyle fits the dream.
7. Thou shalt reward thyself for jobs well done and milestones met.
8. Thou shalt make housework easy to do by organizing for efficiency, because only as work is easily done will we do much of it.
9. Thou shalt find joy in beauty and order. We are not accomplishing these goals for simply utilitarian purposes. Only as we joy in our accomplishments will we be willing to continue.
10. Thou shalt not procrastinate. Keep things up and do jobs as soon as thou shalt notice they need doing. Do not leave it out to be put up later.

23

Energy

The Spark Plug of Housekeeping

Fatigue makes cowards of us all.

Vince Lombardi

In the book of Proverbs (31:17), Solomon states about the ideal woman, "She girdeth her loins with strength, and strengtheneth her arms." Apparently this woman knew some way to strengthen herself deliberately. There are ways we too can find energy to do our work.

Think Ahead about Adjustments

As we work we can conserve what energy we have by wearing comfortable shoes, such as nurses or waitresses wear. Or buy good quality athletic shoes.

If you work outside the home, make sure you do all you can to arrive home at the end of the day as strong as possible. If you must stand in one place all day, buy a spongy rug to prevent fatigue of the feet and legs. If possible, use air-conditioning or bring your own fan if circumstances allow.

When I taught math, I used only a fan when it was not too warm because the air conditioner made it necessary for me to talk louder, which exhausted me. Instead of standing to write on the chalkboard, I sat on a stool and used an overhead projector on which I could write without moving from my stool. This had the added advantage of permitting me to face the class while I wrote, so I was able to keep an eye on my students. This is how I solved some of my energy-draining problems. Can you think of adjustments you can make to save some of your energy?

Eat for Energy

Another source of energy is nutrition. My daughter's miniature horse, Wild Thing, lives in a fenced-off section of our yard. When we first got the horse she had been eating sweet feed, a high-energy food. The veterinarian recommended that she should be switched to rolled oats because sweet feed gave her too much energy, and that would not be good for her in the somewhat confined area in which she lives. If rolled oats had proved to be too energy-producing we could have switched to horse pellets, which provide even less energy.

While I am not suggesting that you buy sweet feed, I am suggesting that the same principle applies to people. Find the combination of food that works to make you feel your best. Don't think it will come naturally; it probably won't. You'll have to search for the proper foods.

I have friends who claim that if they miss their vitamins one day, they feel a letdown the next. If vitamins help you, don't neglect them.

Medicine prescribed by a doctor for a special condition should not be overlooked. I take thyroid medicine because my thyroid has been removed. If I were to forget to take the medicine for any length of time or get the idea that I could exist without it, I would be a limp noodle before very long. Many women over fifty suffer from low-grade thyroid dysfunction and don't know it. A quick blood test will diagnose any thyroid problems. Take health seriously, for the sake of your house and yourself.

Spruce Up Your Looks

Perhaps the quickest way to get a surge of energy is to improve your looks! A good haircut at frequent intervals is a must for me. I have heavy hair that tends to be oily. If I let it get long, it becomes heavy and droopy. Then I begin feeling heavy and droopy, too.

Another quick improvement can be made in the area of makeup. Go to beauty advisors either at a cosmetics store or at a better department store. Maybe your local drugstore has a good cosmetics department.

A warning is in order, though. Cosmetics are expensive and it is a good idea to go with some spending limit in mind. Buy a little now and go back for more later if necessary. Check magazine articles and books on makeup. It's a fun and revitalizing pursuit.

Since my house has been organized, my mind has cleared up, too. Now I can give attention to details such as jewelry. I don't dress up every day using accessories, but I am happy to have the right ones when I need them. Previously, things were in such a jumble I had trouble knowing what I had or how to find it.

For those who spend the day at home, there is a temptation to bum around in the same old junky outfits. Buying a new outfit or two will put pep in your step. Getting up early, showering, dressing, putting on some makeup and a new smock, a shorts outfit, or whatever you find best to wear for comfort at work will get the day off to a good start. Dragging around in a gown and robe telegraphs to your body that you are not ready to work yet.

A long-range change in your weight will also produce energy. Too much or too little weight will wear a person out. Not having control of weight discourages improvement of any kind because it makes us feel powerless. Somehow, many people who struggle with keeping too much also tend to gather too much weight.

Losing weight is a long, hard process. Don't wait to put the other suggestions for energy into practice until you lose weight. Be the best you can be, no matter your size.

Value the State of Your Mind

There is one organ of the body that has a great reservoir of energy waiting to be tapped. That organ is the brain. Have you ever noticed that when there is work to be done the body becomes very tired, but if there is fun to be had energy seems to come from nowhere? Having a messy house is tiring. William James said, "Nothing is so fatiguing as the eternal hanging on of uncompleted tasks." He was right! Having all those odds and ends to do makes the day look like an unpleasant mountain to climb. Energy will come from order, and from success in gaining control of the work in the house. You will be buoyed by the order and beauty around you.

Success brings more success, and that brings energy. Three weeks after one of my students started on the program, her husband sent her flowers with a note saying, "The house looks great, Honey!" What do you suppose that did for her energy level?

Build in Valuable Habits

Remember, too, that we all need breaks to keep our energy high. Some of us spend so much time trying to bring order out of chaos in our houses that we don't take any time off for relaxation. We don't feel it is right to play until our work is done. And our work is never done.

Take one day a week for fun. Plan not to work on that day. Then when you get back to work, you'll get a lot more done.

Spiritual faith is another source of strength. In the book of Isaiah we read, "He gives strength to the weary and increases the power of the weak.... Those who hope in the LORD will renew their strength. They will soar on wings like eagles; they will run and not grow weary, they will walk and not be faint" (40:29, 31 NIV). I really feel that much tiredness in housekeeping is tiredness of life as it is. Only if the soul is joyful can the problem be overcome.

Turn Off the Television

I mentioned earlier that I was once hooked on a soap opera. I say *hooked* because I had to structure my day around the soap opera. I could not go out to do errands if I could not get back in time for the program. In short, I found I needed my daily "fix" or I was uncomfortable and hard to get along with.

Then the program was moved to a time when it was not possible for me to watch TV. What an answer to my need! I vowed never to get into that kind of bondage again.

One part of the program I did miss was the beautiful house the characters lived in. The folks were wealthy and had maids. One of the few spots of order and beauty in my life was that soap opera. Now it is much better to have order and beauty in my own house.

Break the soap opera habit. The people in these shows are losers—interesting losers, but losers nonetheless. They are immoral, too, and this is bad input for anybody.

Speaking of immoral losers, jettison the habit of watching the judge shows and talk shows that daily parade what must be the world's worst decision makers. The messes many of these people have made of their lives can't help but drag down any listener's mental outlook.

Good books of the right kind can be motivating and uplifting. But they, like television, require that you take time from your work. So use them sparingly at first if you are inclined to be a book addict.

Reading the Bible or another spiritual work first thing in the morning can lead us into that right relationship with the Lord, from whom we draw strength. My habit is not to let my feet hit the floor in the morning until I have read my Bible and prayed. If you don't know where to start, I suggest the Psalms and the book of John. From there you can branch out on your own or get a good book to guide you at your Christian bookstore.

We have decided. We have organized. Now we have time to paint a few dreams.

24

MA ClutterBuddies

Winners make it happen; losers let it happen.

"You alone can do it, but you can't do it alone." This is a favorite slogan for support groups. Support is a powerful tool to use when you want to make change in your life. If you are living a Messie lifestyle and hating it, you want to make change. Getting a ClutterBuddy, a partner who understands and will support you, can be a tremendous boost. The original support group, Alcoholics Anonymous, was started by two men meeting together to overcome their addiction. Did that ever work out well!

In her book on goal setting called *Wishcraft*, Barbara Sher comments on the buddy system. "The principle is simple: you and a friend make it your shared goal to meet both your individual goals. It works because it's about a thousand times easier to have faith, courage, and good ideas for someone else than it is for yourself—and easier for someone else to have them for you."

If you've tried to clean up your organizational act and failed, don't give up. If you are trying and making discouragingly slow progress, take heart. Help is available. Solomon once said, "Two are better than one; because they have a good reward for their labor. For if they fall, the one will lift up his fellow. But woe to him that is alone when he falleth; for he hath not another to help him up" (Eccles. 4:9–10). Get a buddy. The two of you can do wonders together!

Picking an MA ClutterBuddy

Your MA ClutterBuddy should understand both your strong desire to change and how hard it is. Sometimes it is hard to work with someone who is already close to you because other personal issues interfere, so you will want to take that into consideration if you are thinking of choosing a family member or close friend. The MA ClutterBuddy relationship is a relationship of equals. There is no leader or teacher. Each of you supports the other. It would probably be better if your partner were a Messie too, but that is not necessary. Choose a buddy wisely but don't wait for the perfect one.

Since Messies generally keep their problem a secret, if you don't know another Messie you might want to tell prospects that you want to upgrade your house and are looking for someone else who wants either to do the same or work on some other goal in life. Your buddy does not ever have to come to your house if that is a problem to you. In some cases your partner might be working on other goals like writing a book or starting a business. Each of you is there to keep the other on track and, for you, that is the track to an orderly, beautiful, workable house.

To find an MA ClutterBuddy on the computer join the group called Friends-of-the-Organizer-Lady that you can find on the website www.messies.com. Go to the Online Support Group page.

Dreaming Your Dreams and Going for Them

Messies love to dream of having another place, perhaps an apartment away from everything, where the rooms are cool and beautiful and everything is always in order. But the time has come for the daydreams to lead the way to reality, to the house where you and your family live in which you create beauty and order.

That needs to be done step-by-step. Tell your ClutterBuddy your goals for the week and when you plan to do them. Perhaps you will start the Mount Vernon Method. That's usually the best way to start. Perhaps you will choose another project. Tell your partner how you plan to do it. Each week you set new goals and new strategies for success. When you do that you have a gentle accountability and that makes all the difference.

Sharing the Thrill of Victory and the Agony of Defeat

Some plans will work out; some will not. You need someone to cheer you on when you succeed. You need someone to encourage you when you don't. Sometimes you need a fresh idea when you have run out. One and one makes more than two. Two people together form a third and powerful force for change. Keep your relationship focused on the goal at hand and you will find that the energy created will move you forward in a way you could never have progressed alone.

Barbara Sher comments, "Your buddy isn't your externalized *conscience* so much as the appointed representative of your best self." A part of you wants to change. A part does not. Your buddy helps keep the part that does in control—at least enough of the time to make progress.

Giving You a Practical Boost

Not long ago I went horseback riding in the mountains of Colorado. It was glorious. But I could never have done it if someone had not given me a boost up into the saddle. Sometimes you need a practical boost. It could be to get going or to keep going or to help in a crisis. Sometimes you need someone to come over to the house and advise you how to proceed. You may even get together in each other's house and work side by side. Things look a lot different when you have an objective partner helping you make decisions. Maybe she has some leftover wood you can use for shelves or knows where to buy just the organizational aid you need. Perhaps your ClutterBuddy knows a good, reasonable handyman or cleaning service. You have skills, contacts, and information that she does not, just as she has things that you do not.

The Weekly Business Meeting

Get together each week. This is essential. It is the heart of the buddy system. Before you start, have a get-started meeting in which you discuss your overall goals. Bring pictures if that will help, pictures of your house as it is now or pictures cut out of a magazine of how you want it to look. Dream and plan. Write your goals, both long-term and intermediate. It is better to have several intermediate goals with a time frame for getting them done than just one very long-range goal. Again, don't be perfectionistic. You don't have to hit your time goal, but you will find that you do better if you aim toward it.

Pick a time and place when you both can meet for an hour. Commit yourself to meeting each week unless there is some strong reason why you cannot. In that case, meet over the phone (or by email). You owe it to your partner not to skip a meeting. But more than that you owe it to yourself. Each partner should write down the other's goals. Think about the other during the week. Pray for her success if prayer is part of your life. Make plans to call each other during important parts of the week or call occasionally to see how things are going.

Wishcraft, from which many of these ideas are gleaned, suggests the following:

Be on time. This is a business meeting, not a social hour.
Use a clock or kitchen timer. Each person gets half an hour.

- Five minutes is for reporting what you have accomplished.
- Twenty minutes is for problems and solutions. No more than ten minutes of this time should be spent in grousing and complaining if complaining is really necessary. During this time do not try to solve your partner's problems. Trying to "fix" her problems and getting heavily involved in her emotional issues will not be helpful. Ask her, "What do you want me to do for you about this?"
- The last five minutes should be spent setting up a new schedule for the week. Each partner keeps a record of the other person's schedule and perhaps schedules a booster call during the week.

Evaluate. You may, of course, decide together to change the timing of the meeting, but don't allow it to drift into a social gathering. At intervals, evaluate whether to continue meeting and for how much longer. If you want to chat, plan to do it after the business meeting.

Three-Minute Booster Phone Call

A booster call (or an email) may be scheduled or made spontaneously when you have gone over some big hurdle (such as having a successful family conference about the house or finishing organizing the garage), or when you need help or think your partner might. The point is, it should be a maximum of three minutes and should only be made occasionally unless you schedule something more often for a special purpose.

Glen Evans in *The Family Circle Guide to Self-Help* writes,

> Of course there will be those who make significant improvement in their homes and way of life without being a part of a self-help group. However, experience shows us that some will not improve on their own and that those who could improve by struggling alone will be able to improve more consistently and more permanently with support.

Other Avenues of Help

In addition to the MA ClutterBuddy program, Messies Anonymous offers groups that meet to study the twelve steps of recovery first given by Alcoholics Anonymous. Information about the twelve steps and how to apply them is found in the book *Hope for the Hopeless Messie*, available directly from Messies Anonymous.

Online help is available from the Messies Anonymous webpage (www. messies.com), on which Messies can connect with others for support in recovery. Other help is also available from the webpage.

The Blessing of Abstinence

In Messies Anonymous, we can take advantage of abstinence. It will make our recovery easier. Make your own abstinence list and see if your messy house doesn't begin to benefit. Start with one or two. You may include something like the following.

I will abstain from:

- Dropping things by the front door when I come in
- Eating in the bedroom
- Buying another book until I get rid of one
- Leaving dishes on the table
- Putting papers on the dining room or coffee table

Take advantage of the gift of abstinence. Choose one or two to start with. Share that choice with someone who can support you in implementing it consistently. You'll find your house will make automatic changes as you follow your plan.

PART 5

The Payoff

25

Painting on Your Clean Canvas

*Everybody needs his memories. They keep
the wolf of insignificance from the door.*

SAUL BELLOW

The nice thing about being organized is that it enables you to do what you want to do, to paint what you want on your nice, clean, prepared canvas. This is particularly important for your personal life whether you live alone, with someone else, or in a family. Now you have time to establish your family or individual traditions.

For Singles

If you are single you may think this section is not for you. Tradition is for families, right? Poppycock! I think tradition is even more important for singles to attend to than for families, because in families you have tradition more or less thrust on you by the kids or by your spouse.

If you are single, you are pretty much responsible for your own traditions or lack of them. Some people can carry on traditions for their own sakes. I can't. If I don't have someone to share it with I hardly think it is worthwhile. So I would have to build people into my tradition if I were single. They might be other singles like myself, senior citizens, families, or students.

I knew a single college librarian who regularly invited students to her room for waffles. She had coconut waffles, pecan waffles, all kinds of waffles and syrups. A touch of home cooking meant a lot to us. Students would bring back special waffle toppings from their vacations. I am sure her life was enriched by her tradition. So was ours.

If you are single, don't let what could be very rewarding traditions slip by because of lack of thought.

If you live near your family, many of your traditions will involve them. But don't settle for that. Be imaginative! Start your own!

For Families

With families, traditions are lying around for the taking. Bedtime stories, special foods, birthday parties, and holidays can hardly be avoided.

Some of the hardest things to manage are children's treasures. These are papers, awards, school pictures, and other memorabilia your child brings home. Where can they be kept? The answer is a Treasure Box. This is a box about orange crate size that you can cover with sticky, plastic paper. Inside put manila file folders, one for each year. If you like, you can decorate the outside with the child's picture and name. In each folder put some of the school papers from each year along with certificates and other mementos. There is also room for some of the bulkier treasures of childhood, like the box with the frog skeleton.

Don't overdo. A sample of each thing will be enough to prod the memory. At the end of each school year, let the child help choose.

In the regular flow of family life, some nice everyday traditions can develop now that the house is not holding you back. For example, we like to have family night from time to time. For us it is usually a Friday night. A friend of mine could not come to a meeting one Saturday because she and her husband and teenage son had planned a family day for that Saturday. I like that.

Some Special Day Tips

The problem with traditions is that they require a lot of effort. You have to be organized to keep a good tradition running.

If you put the systems in this book to use, you will have a handle on things. You will know where the Christmas things are; you will know where the Halloween things are. In short, things will be under control.

You will be surprised how knowing where things are can enrich your life. Somehow it gives starch to the mind. Flabby, half-formed ideas will march out in full-dress uniform for your family to enjoy. Things that were just too much bother will be done because now you will have the time and energy to do them.

What are some of these traditions? There are the usual things like displaying the flag on holidays now that you know where the flag is, and there are bedtime stories now that you have all the children's books gathered together.

Special foods from your own ethnic background or traditional family favorites are important. In my family we eat black-eyed peas on New Year's Day and believe the more peas a person eats, the more money he will get. I can't see it has worked all that well for me but it may work for you. A friend of mine adds a unique twist to this tradition. In her family they add a clean silver dime to the dish containing the peas. Whoever gets the dime gets double luck in the new year. They use the same dime year after year.

Then there are birthday celebrations. In the birthday cake you can bake a peanut. Whoever gets the piece with the peanut gets a special prize. Let the birthday celebrant be the one to select the menu for that night. Recently we have added another aspect to birthday celebrations. At the table we each tell what we most appreciate about the person whose special day it is and then we give him or her a Bible verse.

Thanksgiving and New Year's are at the beginning and end of the big holiday season of the year. I think Thanksgiving is my favorite holiday because of the purely personal relationship between God and me couched in the context of national thanksgiving.

Christmas

It is a good thing that Thanksgiving comes first, giving strength for the days to come until New Year's. Of course Christmas is the highlight of the season for us as a family.

You really have to be organized to have a satisfying and joyful Christmas. First you have to know where the Christmas things are stored. Hopefully they are all together in boxes labeled "Christmas" and stacked alphabetically in the garage, basement, or attic. If they are not, you should have the places where they are stored listed on your computer or in your box under the special heading "Storage" so that you can find them when preparation for the big day comes.

Buying presents, putting up decorations, and cooking are the big three of Christmas celebration. Gift buying is best handled by spreading it out through the year so that by the time December 25 comes you are ready.

It is also a good idea to wrap each gift as you buy it so that you are not hiding in the back room on Christmas Eve wrapping gifts by yourself when it would be nicer to enjoy time with the family in the living room. Put the names of the people for whom you are going to buy gifts during the year in the monthly section of your box at the beginning of the month in which you plan to buy them.

Decorations come out from year to year and carry more importance because of the memories tied in with them. The star you lifted three-year-old Johnny to put on the tree he now puts up himself because he's the only one tall enough to reach the treetop.

Christmas tree balls are the most important of decorations. One of the saddest experiences of my early married life was the first Christmas my husband and I spent together alone. When the time came to put up the tree, a little blue tabletop one, we had to go out to a store to buy decorations. There they dangled, strange Christmas balls, hung by string instead of metal hooks, since I fancied we were too poor to buy metal hooks. As a result of that experience, I decided my kids would have their own Christmas balls, with heavy tradition attached, to take into their own homes.

So each Christmas I buy four matching balls. One ball is for my husband and me to keep. The other three are for each of our three children. If possible we mark the year in an unseen place on the ornament and include the name of the child if it is hard to tell one ornament from the other. Other ornaments we give our children were made by them at nursery school. Some we painted on summer vacations at the cabin. I guess it is too much to hope that the young people our children marry will bring a similarly collected selection of Christmas ornaments to be merged on the tree for their first Christmas together.

We still come across a Christmas ball now and again with a string attached instead of a metal hook. So even that first sad experience became a Christmas memory of the bittersweet kind.

Christmas foods tend to run in families. A special kind of turkey dressing, a favorite eggplant casserole, all are happily anticipated before they are actually enjoyed.

For a great book on Christmas, get *Take Joy* by Tasha Tudor. When you open the book you can practically hear the jingle of sleigh bells and smell the Christmas cookies baking. It has songs, recipes, and best of all, loads of tradition. And when you have your house clean and neat, your storage under control, and your time planned, you can enjoy these traditions too. I bet Tasha Tudor is a Cleanie. One of the nice ideas she suggests is the Kris Kringle tradition. In her family, around December 12, they each draw a name of a family member secretly. During the days between then and Christmas, it is each Kris Kringle's job to do nice little things in secret for his or her special person. On Christmas Eve each person tries to guess who his or her Kris Kringle was, and the secret is revealed.

Church

I was talking to my daughter about our family traditions that had plugged along enthusiastically if not efficiently during my Messie years. She enjoyed the ones I mentioned, but she was really enthusiastic about our traditional church activities.

I realize that not all churches provide the same support for the individual and family in spiritual and social ways as ours does. Our church is a kind of extended family, and the people are warm and genuinely interested in each other. They contribute a lot to our family.

It is important for us to get up and go to church. On Sunday morning, I like to keep the same schedule of popping out of bed, doing the dailies, eating breakfast, and getting off, leaving the house tidy in case somebody should come home with us.

If it is too much effort to make a big breakfast, have sweet rolls and sausage served on paper plates and let the children drink out of plastic cups. Throw the plates and cups away after use and you are ready to go.

From my personal standpoint, the Sunday morning church service is the highlight of my week. And it is much easier to go and really enjoy it if the house is in order and ready to send me off and welcome me back. It leaves me in a good frame of mind so I can relax and enjoy the day. Because I feel good about the order that is around me, I feel good about myself, and I am able to look forward to the fresh, clean canvas of a new week.

Family Traditions

Old Christmas decorations are the prettiest. New ones picked out or made by a child come next. Plastic ones fall short, unless they carry the baby's tooth marks.

For boys, enormous gift packages are the best. Middle-sized ones that rattle come next. Anything that looks like it came from a clothing store doesn't count.

For girls, tiny boxes from the jewelry store are the best. Middle-sized ones that rattle come next. Some years, even boxes from the clothing store count.

The Fourth of July needs a parade and a cookout. It doesn't need rain. It definitely doesn't need the thought of summer school.

26

The Real Beginning for You

One finds one's way only by taking it.

A. D. SERTILLANGES

You now know just about everything I know about how to leave the morass of messiness for an ordinary life.

I struggled for twenty-three years to play the housekeeping game, and for twenty-three years I lost. The methods I have shared with you have changed my life. They can change yours, too, if you choose to put what you have learned into action.

First, recognize that you are a Messie but that it is not necessary to live like one. It is possible to move up the scale. Commit yourself to becoming a successful average housekeeper and then analyze yourself to see just exactly which habits are creating the most difficulty for you.

Next, set some short- and some long-range goals for yourself, and use the Mount Vernon Method to organize your home. Be sure to discard everything that isn't useful or beautiful. Take your time and save your energy, because the changes you are about to undergo will revolutionize your life.

Once your house is organized and free of the accumulation of the years, purchase the necessary tools to keep it that way. Always remember that procrastination can defeat you, and use your tools as effective weapons against it.

Involve your family in your endeavors and remember that it may take them some time to adjust to your efforts.

The plan works. It works marvelously, but only if you make it work. You must sprinkle the magic dust. I'd love to hear from you to know of your successes.

I wish you well. May God bless you as you begin to set and accomplish your goals. Join me and the throng of organized Messies who are extremely grateful for the release we have found from our former cluttered way of life.

In the end, coming to terms with the fact that in order to change we must give up our old habits, our cherished ideas, and our comforting "things" will be the determining factor in whether we will be successful in finding an orderly and harmonious life for ourselves.

Appendix

Ideas That Work

Motivating Yourself

Inspire enthusiasm—Have one or two things in your house that focus your interest and enthusiasm—like a shiny toaster, a sparkling bathroom, or whatever fuels your energy.

Do it for others—Invite company over regularly. Nothing helps you to see what needs to be done better than knowing that guests will come and see your house from a fresh perspective. We tend to see the house from their standpoint when we know they are coming.

Get a cleaner—Consider professional help. Wouldn't it be nice, after you have gotten organized, to have a cleaning professional come in and give the house a special cleaning? If you stay home while she is there, you can tackle some big job you haven't had time for and *really* have the house sparkling. Somehow it's easier to work when there's somebody else working too.

Switch jobs—Mop the floor of a friend and have him or her clean your stove. Somehow it isn't as hard to do someone else's house.

Have a cleaning party—Invite a friend over to sit with you and talk, or to help you, when you are cleaning or doing a special task like organizing a closet. The friend will help encourage you to throw things away. ("Will I need this, Jane? Naw, probably not. I'll throw it away.") Then stop long enough to put things away. Go out to lunch together or eat the special lunch you fixed the night before to celebrate.

Work with a time limit—Do a job by time. Set the timer on your stove, or better still, put on a CD. Plan to work for only two or three songs. You may find that once you start you'll go on for a while longer.

If you have a big job, put on a Marine Band album or the "1812 Overture." That will give you enough time and enthusiasm for a huge job.

Give yourself rewards—Reward yourself for a job well done. Food is a good reward if you're skinny. Even if you're not, there are some very good foods, like artichokes and crabmeat, that are real treats and not fattening. A piece of jewelry, a day with a friend, or an extravagant soap will do nicely.

Let one success lead to another—Success is the biggest motivator. Once things are under control, beautiful, and convenient, you will not want to return to the old way again. The compliments of family and friends are the fuel that fires our minds, hearts, and bodies. And then there is that bottom line: we like the new way better ourselves.

Still More Tips for Organizing

Several sensible ideas will keep your house moving in the right direction:

One room, one purpose—Make it a point to use each room for the function for which it was designed. This means don't take off your shoes in the living room and don't eat in the bedroom. Plan to eat in the dining room or kitchen and undress in the bedroom.

Stand it up—There is more air space than surface space, so it is a good idea to stand up anything that can stand up rather than lay it on a table, desk, chair, or sofa.

This is particularly true of magazines. If you have several special issues, make a magazine holder from a cereal box. Cover the cereal box with woodgrain Con-Tact paper. It will look like a library box. Then place the magazines in it and put it on a bookshelf so that magazines are standing up instead of lying down.

If your drawers are crowded, consider hanging up your nightgowns or anything that can be hung up. This is the same principle in a different form.

Automate—If you know of any automatic products, use them. Some examples are fertilizer spikes that fertilize the plants so you don't have to do it so often. Purchase new cleaners that you can put in the toilet tank to clean the toilet automatically. Use anything that will lengthen the time between essential jobs.

Start early—For most people an ounce of morning is worth a pound of afternoon.

Also remember:

> Early to bed, early to rise,
> Makes your house neater than otherwise.

It's this attitude that gets most Cleanies off to such a good start in the morning. So get up, get dressed, and get going.

General Hints

Ring-around-the-collar—Use shampoo on collar and cuff rings. Shampoo is meant to clean body oil, which is what that ring is.

Window cleaning—Use a squeegee and an appropriate spray. This is the easiest way. Also use a squeegee on the walls of your shower. It will keep water spots and soap deposits from building up.

Keeping up with things—Are you forgetful? Do you leave things lying around? Write your name, address, and phone number on all your small notebooks and other easy-to-lose possessions.

Vinyl—Don't put oil on vinyl to make it soft and shiny. It will eventually harden it and cause it to split. There are good vinyl protectors on the market. Grocery stores, drugstores, and auto supply stores carry them.

Storing sheets—When you fold your sheets, fold the sheets and the pillowcases in one bundle, with the flat sheet covering them all. Then you can grab the whole set to be put on the bed with one hand.

Bathroom fixtures—Use liquid cleanser on bathroom fixtures because powdered cleansers dull the finish. If you have a very dirty sink or tub and feel you must use a powder, use Dutch Cleanser, Zud, or Bon Ami, since they have milder abrasives than most.

Leftovers—Put a list of leftovers on the refrigerator door. Cross them off as they are used.

Plastic ice trays—Don't wash these in warm water. You will remove something that keeps the ice from sticking. If you have already washed them in hot water, coat them lightly with cooking oil spray to restore the slick surface.

Waxing the bathroom—You can use car wax to polish and wax bathroom fixtures (not the inside of the tub, please). You can also use other furniture polish to wax the ceramic tile if you wish. Just be sure that wax does not make any area in the bathroom slippery.

Shelf lining—Use the heaviest shelf paper you can locate to line your shelves. If you have a kitchen cabinet that has an open space above the top cabinet, be sure to cover this or it will get really dirty and greasy.

Dirty tub—Clean it right after using, before body oil has a chance to harden. You can even start the cleaning while you are in the tub. Don't use slippery cleanser while you are still in the tub though. Don't use any harsh cleanser on any tub made before 1964. It will remove the finish. Believe me, I speak from firsthand experience.

Vacuum easier—Use an upright vacuum. The uprights are so much easier to put away and get out that you will be inclined to vacuum more often because it's not "too much trouble" to get this kind of vacuum out for a little job. If you have an upstairs, keep one of the lightweight upright vacuums that can be hung from the wall in an upstairs closet on the second floor for easy access.

Resources

When I first searched for help with my organizing problems, there was precious little available. I found myself in the archives of a university library reading about how to remove the starch from the plate of my iron and how to catch the dripping water from my icebox. Not too helpful.

Things are different today—we have come a long way. Now we are awash with wonderful books about organizing many different aspects of our lives. They are flowing nonstop. But that leaves us Messie people with a problem. Which ones to buy?

There are two kinds of books on organizing. The first group is those written by people who are super organized and just love to write about how to become even more organized. These straight-laced books will drive disorganized people crazy if they try to superimpose them on their topsy-turvy world and way of doing things. However, they can be useful windows into another way of life. They are truly eyepoppers. The shock of seeing how organized people think may even jolt us into a different reality and jump-start us into action. "You mean people really live like this?"

The more useful books for us are those by basically disorganized writers who talk the language of Messies because these writers have struggled with and overcome the problem. Since the writers are often creative, right-brained folks, the books are often fun to read and offer practical approaches that work for their struggling readers.

Now we come to the important questions. How many of these books should you get and which ones? The answer is as many as it takes to get the job done. Browse through them at the library or bookstore and choose the ones that appeal to you most. If this one helped you, you may want to get my other books. Disorganized people often have many books on organizing. Remember, although books can be invaluable, they don't work unless you read and begin to apply them. For many people they work best as a part of a total program that includes outside support from a professional, self-help group, internet group, MA ClutterBuddy, or all of the above.

Where do you get these books? Browse the bookstore, internet, or library. New books are coming out every day. Log on to www.messies.com for a list of the books we offer. Find the book that appeals to your needs and your way of thinking. Get one that offers a plan and follow that plan. Later get other books that can reinspire you and help you upgrade your system. Don't try to implement everything from everyone. You'll go nuts. One of the Messies Anonymous slogans is "Keep It Simple."

Organizing the House

Aslett, Don. *Clutter Free, Finally and Forever*. 1995. The title pretty much says it all. Anything by Don Aslett is likely to be useful and written in a sprightly way.

Campbell, Jeff. *Clutter Control*. 1994. Guidelines for uncluttering.

Culp, Stephanie. *How to Conquer Clutter*. 1990. Useful A–Z format. If you want help on any specific organizing problem, look up the letter it begins with and it is there.

Eisenbert, Ronni. *Organize Yourself!* 1997. Straightforward, detailed, and thorough. A good resource.

Felton, Sandra. The Flipper. Revised and expanded in 1998. An organizational system that includes a booklet, flip-card album with cards, audiotape, and special pen for marking off tasks.

————. *Messie No More.* 1989. Why are some of us disorganized and others are not? This book looks into the underlying Messie mind-sets and suggests ideas to overcome them.

————. *The Messies Superguide: Strategies and Ideas for Conquering Catastrophic Living.* 1987. Explores a right-brained approach to organizing. Gentle, encouraging, and helpful. Contains specific how-tos and suggestions.

Kolberg, Judith. *Conquering Chronic Disorganization.* 1998. Unique methods for putting disorganization behind you compatible with your personal organizing style.

Lockwood, Georgene. *The Complete Idiot's Guide to Organizing Your Life.* 1996. Breezy, fun, and very informative. If you like the practical info the Idiot's Guide books are known for, you should get this one.

Winston, Stephanie. *Getting Organized.* 1991. A classic, recently revised. You can't go wrong on this one whether you are a man or woman. Anything, including *The Organized Executive*, 1994, by Stephanie Winston will be solid material.

Paper Clutter

Culp, Stephanie. *Conquering the Paper Pile-Up.* 1990. How to sort, organize, file, and store every piece of paper in your home and office.

Hemphill, Barbara. *Taming the Paper Tiger at Home.* 1998. One of the best when it comes to handling paper.

Organizing Offices—Home or Business

Hemphill, Barbara. *Taming the Paper Tiger at Work.* 2002. Covers many aspects of getting organized at work, including working from home and business, on the road, going to conventions, etc.

Kanarek, Lisa. *Organizing Your Home Office for Success.* 1993. Step-by-step guide to all aspects of home offices. Also check out her book *101 Home Office Success Secrets.* 1993.

Mayer, Jeffrey. *Winning the Fight between You and Your Desk.* 1993. A book on using your computer most effectively to organize your office.

Pollar, Odette. *Organizing Your Workspace.* 1993. Ideas that can be applied to home or business office.

Zbar, Jeff. *Going SOHO (Small Office, Home Office).* 1998. Practical fifty-two pages written by a journalist who works from home and knows what he's talking about. This booklet has a good appendix with websites for home office users.

The Family and Organizing

Dobson, James. *The New Dare to Discipline.* 1999. An update on a classic on child rearing with a Christian outlook. Check out another of Dr. Dobson's books, *The Strong-Willed Child.*

Felton, Sandra. *When You Live with a Messie.* 1994. If a disorganized person is seriously complicating your cleanup efforts, this is the book for you. Tough, yet gentle. Keep your relationship while keeping house the way you want it to be.

Sprinkle, Patricia. *Children Who Do Too Little*. 1993. This book is for your own good. But mostly it is for the good of your children so they will be able to take care of themselves and others when they grow up. It is a heartwarming, no-nonsense, practical approach to what can be a great gift you can give your children.

There are many new books coming out all the time. Go to your favorite bookstore and browse noting those that deal with family teamwork around the house.

Cleaning Up

Aslett, Don. *Make Your House Do the Housework*. 1995. Don Aslett is also a professional cleaner. He has loads of books on cleaning. Don't overdo but if you need instruction on cleaning, he's got it.

Campbell, Jeff, and the Clean Team. *Spring Cleaning*. 1989. How to do big jobs that you may or may not ever wish to do. Written with the expertise of a professional cleaner. Keep in mind Jeff's other books: *Speed Cleaning*, 1991; *Clutter Control*, 1992; *Talking Dirt*, 1997.

Time Management

Aslett, Don. *How to Have a 48 Hour Day*. 1996. This sounds like a tiring prospect, but the focus is on increasing your productivity. Discusses lists, schedules, and priorities along with other time-related factors.

Culp, Stephanie. *Streamline Your Life, A 5-Point Plan for Uncomplicated Living.* 1991. Always pointed and energetic, they infuse the reader with resolve. Stephanie has a whole bunch of other books on organizing, many of which have to do with time management. Check them out.

Lakein, Alan. *How to Get Control of Your Time and Your Life.* 1996. A classic in time management for good reason. Excellent suggestions.

MacKenzie, Alec. *Time Trap.* 1996 revision. Another classic on self-management. Discusses twenty biggest time wasters and how to overcome them.

McGee-Cooper, Ann. *Time Management for Unmanageable People.* 1993. Fun, a little zany, designed for right-brained people. Very helpful.

Other Contributing Factors

Attention Deficit Disorder

Felton, Sandra. *Why Can't I Get Organized? Success Strategies for Those with Attention Deficit Disorder and Other Distractible Folks* and *The Whiz Bang Guide on How to Organize Time and Things.* 1998. The first book explains how ADD interferes with organization and gives an overview of organizing techniques that work for distractible people. The second book offers specific tips, products, and approaches that do the trick in organizing for ADDers.

Hartman, Thom. *ADD Success Stories.* 1995. Contains helpful coping information from individuals with ADD. His 1997 book, *Attention Deficit Disorder: A Different Perspective,* offers an encouraging approach to the problem of ADD.

Hollowell, Edward, and John J. Ratey. *Driven to Distraction: Recognizing and Coping with Attention Deficit Disorder from Childhood through Adulthood.* 1993. One of the classics in the area of attention deficit disorder (ADD). This book gives an excellent overview of the problem, diagnosis, medication, and coping skills including organizing.

Snowdon, Suzanne. *Aim High: Gameplanning for ADD/LD.* 1996. This is an important resource guide for ADD services and products.

Solden, Sari. *Women with Attention Deficit Disorder: Embracing Disorganization at Home and in the Workplace.* 1995. An encouraging book for women containing insights into and help for disorganization.

Obsessive-Compulsive Disorder (OCD)

Unfortunately, not much has been written on the hoarding aspect of OCD. Occasionally a book may mention it briefly. However, anybody who keeps too much stuff mindlessly will likely benefit from this approach whether or not they are diagnosed with OCD. The research of Randy Frost at Smith College in Northampton, Massachusetts, and others in the OCD field may open the doors to more information on the problem of hoarding.

Felton, Sandra. *I've Got to Get Rid of This Stuff: Strategies for Overcoming Hoarding (The Packrat Syndrome).* 1995. Twenty-four pages. A three-week program for people who struggle with clutter and are serious about overcoming their "addiction" to stuff. Excellent techniques. To order log on to www.messies.com.

Organizing Websites and Addresses

Attention Deficit Disorder

ADDA—Attention Deficit Disorder Association website. Lots of user-friendly information about ADD. Articles, books, research, and other websites. www.add.org

CHADD (Children and Adults with Attention Deficit Disorders). www.chadd.org

Online providers—Call your provider if you have trouble accessing ADD information.

America Online: Choose "People Connection/Live Discussions." Access ADD topics from there. Connect to others with ADD and with noted experts.

Compuserve: Attention Deficit Disorder Forum. Go to Services, request Hyperactivity, and go to Attention Deficit Disorder.

Prodigy: Supplies ADD bulletin board help that can be accessed in various ways depending on your interest.

Obsessive-Compulsive Disorder

Association for the Advancement of Behavior Therapy
email: Referral@aabt.org
website: www.aabt.org/aabt
Has fact sheet series including OCD and ADD.

Obsessive-Compulsive Foundation
676 State Street
New Haven, CT 06511
http://ocfoundation.org

The Anxiety Disorders Association of America
6000 Executive Blvd. Suite 200
Rockville, MD 20852-3081
301-231-9350

Families

Focus on the Family—A many-faceted outreach for assisting
   with family problems and encouraging family harmony. Fea-
   turing Dr. James Dobson. http://family.org

Professional Organizers

National Association of Professional Organizers—This organization has access to over one thousand professional organizers. www.napo.net

Professional Organizers' Web Ring.
www.organizerswebring.com

National Study Group on Chronic Disorganization

www.nsgcd.org

Self-Help Groups

Log on to www.messies.com for more information about local
   and online support groups.

Sandra Felton, The Organizer Lady™, is the author of many books on bringing order and beauty to the home, including the bestselling *Messie No More*. She is founder and president of Messies Anonymous, a group for those who seek a new and better way of life. Through her encouragement and information, many have found relief and brought organization and harmony to their lives, homes, and family life.

The purpose of Messies Anonymous is to help people move from a lifestyle of out-of-control clutter to a life of productive and satisfying order. Among the ways that people find help are twelve-step self-help groups, the MA ClutterBuddy program, a quarterly newsletter, and an interactive website (www.messies.com).

Some books written by Sandra Felton that are available through Messies Anonymous are:

* *Time Management for the Harried Teacher*
* *Hope for the Hopeless Messie*
* *Stop Messing Around and Organize to Write*
* *Why Can't I Get Organized?* (for ADHD readers)
* *The Whiz Bang Guide on How to Organize Time and Things*

Audio- and videotapes are also available. For a free introductory newsletter and other information about Messies Anonymous, write MA, 5025 SW 114 Ave., Miami, FL 33165 or log on to www.messies.com.

Funny and practical, Sandra enjoys bringing her powerful message of organizational control to business and professional groups, mental health organizations, church women's ministries, and Christian gatherings through seminars and other meetings. If you would like Sandra to serve as a speaker, you may contact her directly at:

Sandra Felton
5025 SW 114 Ave.
Miami, FL 33165
(305) 271-8404
www.messies.com

Turn the **chaos of your home** into the **castle of your dreams.**

Discover the key to turning a chaotic house into a clutter-free home in no time at all!